THE STERLING COOKBOOK

THE STERLING COOK-BOOK

JACK STERLING

with Dan Morris To Do the Dishes

Funk & Wagnalls NEW YORK

CONTENTS

INTRODUCTION

In 1948 a young announcer, unknown to the East, arrived in New York from Chicago to succeed the hottest name in radio, Arthur Godfrey, on WCBS—the toughest assignment in show business. Twenty years later Jack Sterling is still around, still broadcasting each morning and still one of Big Town's biggest names. He was the voice of the morning on WCBS for eighteen years, and is now in his second year as morning man for WHN.

For more years than either Jack or I care to remember, he's been getting up at the ghastly hour of 3:15 A.M. to commute into Manhattan from his home in New Canaan, Connecticut, go on the air from 6 to 10 o'clock, then attend sales meetings and business luncheons, make personal appearances and go home every night to his wife, Barbara, and their six lovely daughters. That's quite a show in itself.

Jack follows the same routine every day, except now, so help me, he has added something new. He has ventured into the literary field and written *The Sterling Cookbook*. This is no ordinary cookbook. For one thing, Jack began compiling it, though somewhat unconsciously, almost from the time he was born. Jack's parents were show business troupers, and good ones, too. The vaude team of Jack Sexton and Edna Cable is still remembered by many. Actually, Jack made his debut on the stage at the age of 2 in *East Lynne*.

What has all this got to do with a cookbook? Well, Jack's father was an amateur cook, and he was the one who got Jack interested in cooking almost as soon as he got young Jack started in show business. As a result, all the while Jack was plying his stage trade, he kept sticking his culinary nose into the kitchens of some famous and not-so-famous restaurants around the country (he's on excellent terms with the chefs) and showing more than passing interest in the favorite dishes of show business folk. (You'll find Louis "Satchmo" Armstrong's red beans and rice in here somewhere.)

Today Jack is far more than just a kitchen-putterer-around. His friends will attest to the fact that he's a helluva chef. In Jack's home is a marvelous collection of cookbooks and copper cookware, and the kitchen is a gourmet's mecca. (Jack's own favorite dish is far from exotic—spare ribs. Recipe on pages 101–102.) With all this you'd think the big guy—he's six foot and almost 200 pounds—would have an appetite to match. He does. You should see him, as I have, downing a "snack" after eighteen holes at the Westchester Country Club.

He's a very unusual person, this Jack Sterling, and his book is unusual, too. It's a grand mixture of recipes from friends in show business, simmered with old theatrical boarding house dishes and actors' restaurant menus, and flavored with the creations of all those chefs he's been cultivating since he was the guy we all thought couldn't fill Arthur Godfrey's shoes back in '48.

Jack's blended it all together with an amusing and tasty narrative that should have his publishers alerted for an instant second printing. They'll need it if the book is as good as Jack is . . . and it is. I know. I've already read the galley proofs. That's one of the benefits of writing the introduction.

Ed Sullivan

THE
FOOD
I
LIKE

1

THE EARLY DAYS

My hair may be streaked with gray, I may be a bit rounder in the middle than I ought to be, I may not be able to do a buck and wing as once I did, but I'm not an old man. Still, though, I've been a cook of sorts for more than forty years now, going back to the Roaring Twenties, the Jazz Age. Every one of us here in America lived entirely different lives back in those days, but I doubt that anyone's life could have been more different than mine. That's because, you see, I was one of the Chosen People, a member of a Theatrical Family. Looking back, I see my boyhood as one memorable milestone after another. And one of the most memorable of all was my first encounter with a stove. It wasn't much of a stove, as I recall, but it gave me the bug. I was about seven when my father introduced me to it, rousing me from a warm cot to tell me in his most vaudevillian tone that it was time I started cooking.

It was a Sunday morning, and what he said specifically was that Mother worked hard all week and the least we men could do was to let her sleep late on the Sabbath. We grabbed our meals where we could, how we could and best we could in those days, and it was indeed rare for our Sunday morning breakfast to be cooked on the same stove as the Sunday before. One week we might be in a hotel room, the next week in a rooming house or under canvas or in a trailer or, on those rare occasions when bookings kept us in one town

3

for more than a week or two, in the luxury of a two- or three-room flat.

Mother and Dad griped about some of the places in which we had to stay, but never about what brought them there. Sure, they were in show business to earn a living, but it was more than a living that they derived from it. Show business was their life, their love. They ate it, slept it, drank it. They glorified in it. But they never forgot that we were a family—Mother, Dad, my kid sister Betty and me. We were together always. First there was musical comedy, then vaudeville, stock, show boats and finally tent shows. But we were always together, a family. Every day of the week while Betty and I were too young for school, every day of the summer after that.

We must have stayed in a thousand places, a thousand towns, hundreds of rooming houses, and rarely for more than a week in any one spot. But wherever we were, big city or small town, somehow Mother made every one of those rooming houses a home. And, on Sunday, Dad and I cooked. That's how I developed a love for cooking. Today, with years of show business under my belt and a house on a Connecticut hill and six youngsters—all girls—to help me in my very own kitchen, the bug has still got me. Not even twenty consecutive years of getting up at 3 A.M. to do "The Jack Sterling Radio Show" in New York could crush it.

I like to play golf, I like to fish, I like to play the drums—but I *love* to cook. And I owe it all to Dad. He gave me my first lessons in all of these activities, and he taught me the difference between good food, bad food and food that's passable.

Simple as it seems, bacon is an example. It's one of the easiest things there is to cook, and yet it is seldom cooked properly. It takes more than the ability to toss it into a frying pan and take it out again. That, my Dad told me, is all right if you're satisfied to eat bacon that's only passably good. But, he said, for bacon to be really good it has to be crisp. Not only for taste, but for health reasons too. The crisper it is, the less fatty it is and the healthier you are. The way I crispen it is this: First, I let the bacon stand at room temperature just long enough to be able to separate the strips without breaking. Then I warm up my frying pan—a heavy one—at medium heat. I lay the strips of bacon in it, flat and not touching. I leave the heat at medium, and turn the bacon once or twice. I drain off the grease occasionally, and I keep alert for that moment when the bacon is a rich golden brown. That's when I transfer it gently, slice by slice, to a couple of sheets of absorbent paper to get rid of the excess grease. Dad taught me this when I was very young, and I in turn taught this to my daughters, along with a lot of other culinary cues that I learned from him in those early days.

Don't get the idea that all Dad could do was cook. Once he had stopped working on the railroad, show business was his world, his life. Cooking was his relaxation. Oldtimers who remembered vaudeville and the days of musical comedy troupes will remember the Garden City Four. That was Dad (who was a clerk on the Baltimore & Ohio Railroad) and three other guys who got together every Saturday night in the local pub and sang for only one reason—because they liked to sing. Then someone suggested that they enter an amateur contest. They did and they won. A theatrical booking went with the gold cup, and that's when Dad quit working on the railroad.

A year later he met a chorus girl. Their bookings jelled and so did they. The two were married on stage in a tank-town Pennsylvania theatre after the curtain rang down on that night's performance of *H.M.S. Pinafore* (Dad played Dick Deadeye).

I joined the act two years later, making my debut in a theatrical boarding house in Baltimore. Mother laid over for all of five weeks to have me, and then the three of us were making the circuit again. My actual stage debut was as a babe in arms in *East Lynne;* by the time I was two I had walk-on parts . . . usually with a bottle in my hands, my diapers falling down, completely unexpected and completely unannounced. They tell me the audiences loved it, and I, ham that I am, loved it. (See Roasted Ham recipe on pages 96–97.)

My bed at the theatre was a Taylor trunk, and our home changed every week. The rooms where we stayed at each stopover were pretty much determined by the critiques scrawled on the backstage callboards by previous acts.

"Mrs. Murphy's pitch till you win is tops," a message might say, or "Stay away from Mrs. Clancy's, her gravy is slipping this year," or comments like that. ("Pitch till you win" is a carnival phrase used to describe a game in which the customers pitch rings until they win a prize. But in theatrical boarding house parlance it meant the food—served family style—was both plentiful and good and you could eat until you could eat no more.)

Years later, at family get-togethers when Mother and Dad were still alive, they loved to reminisce about those early days, and sooner or later they'd tell stories about pitch-till-you-win eating and me and my appetite. There's one story about not only me but Dad, too, that Mother never failed to tell, and out of it came two of the recipes you'll find in this book.

We were stopping over at an excellent boarding house run by a woman who not only set the best table in the town but also had a six-year-old daughter who couldn't keep her mouth shut. Every night the menu was the same, but never monotonous because Mrs. Murphy didn't serve just one entree. She piled three platters high, one with roast beef, one with chicken, and one with pork chops and a very special gravy. Then there was a fourth platter loaded down with baking powder biscuits. When one platter ran dry, the landlady would be right there to fill it up again.

The way Mother told the story, Dad had eyes only for the pork chops and gravy soaked up in biscuits and, though my stomach wasn't nearly as big as his, my eyes certainly were. I struggled mightily to keep up, thinking, "Skip the roast beef, skip the chicken, let's empty that pork chop platter." Then I waited hungrily for the landlady to take it out to the kitchen and fill it up again.

We kept her too busy to sit down and eat with us and the other acts boarding in her house. But her daughter did join us at the table and apparently sat popeyed every night just watching in awe as Dad and I dug in. Along about our fifth night there, the lady of the house came in with her third platterful of pork chops and another pan full of hot biscuits and asked, "Is everything all right?" The little girl piped up for everyone to hear, "My God, Mommy, watch that man and that little boy dragging down the biscuits and the pork chops!"

But Dad was a real trouper, quick on the uptake. "Yes, Madam," he said. "You see, my son and I are gourmets in search of recipes. Would you be so good as to oblige?"

She did, and you'll find the recipes on pages 119–121 just as Mrs. Murphy gave them to Dad. She used one ingredient that's a natural for pork chops, yet in all my years I've never seen it mentioned in any cookbook. Plain old everyday apple cider! Try it, and you'll know why Dad and I considered that boarding house one of the best pitch-till-you-win places we ever stayed at.

Living out of a trunk, vaudevillians never did have many creature comforts. So they had to make the most out of the few pleasures available to them, and eating was then, as it is now, one of the most pleasurable. Acts leaving a town would pass the word to acts coming in via the callboard.

I don't imagine anyone paid more attention to those bulletins than did Mother and Dad. Traveling with two children and anxious to give them as much family life as possible, they had to do so. As I recall, some of those boarding house ladies were like second mothers to Betty and me. But others . . . Mother and Dad got out of that kind of place fast.

Every chance they got, my parents would rent a small apartment for a week. These players, of course, had stoves. And Dad taught me to cook, just as Mother taught Betty. They believed that it never was too early for children to learn their way around a recipe. I guess it's another aspect of family togetherness. But, whatever it is and whatever the reason, it rubbed off. Barbara and I bring our youngsters into the cooking act just as Mother and Dad did. Some of the Sunday morning breakfast tricks that Dad taught me, I now teach them. Bacon and eggs were the first things that I learned to cook, not only because they're traditional breakfast fare but also because they're easy for a child to prepare. That's why I began by teaching my brood "bacon-eggs."

I remember, too, Dad impressing on me even then that bacon is a marvelous addition to any number of dishes; for example, Dad's German Hot Potato Salad on page 83.

He had special little tricks for just about every food he touched —even so prosaic a dish as scrambled eggs. He made them far from ordinary with two very simple steps described in the recipe on pages 165–166. Not only is the finished dish satisfying to the appetite and to the taste, but the step-by-step preparations for cooking scrambled eggs are good training for children. Maybe that's why Dad began to teach me to cook by having me help out at breakfast. And just as important, as Dad proved with me, cooking is a good lesson in paying attention to detail. It taught me discipline and self-reliance, too. And now that I am a parent, I can say that no parent with a fondness for cooking can go wrong by bringing their youngsters into the act.

Looking back after all these years, I'd say that many of the things Dad taught me about cooking helped me considerably when I ventured on my own into the wonderful world of show business. I played the drums; I twirled a walking stick and a straw hat in song-and-dance routines—all of them actions that call for nimble fingers, dexterity. And it was Dad who taught me not to be clumsy-fingered, using so simple a prop as an English muffin to do it. To taste as they should, Dad told me, muffins should be broken open by hand. They should never be sliced with a knife, because that causes the muffin to lose its flaky quality and become rubbery. He showed me how to grip a muffin around the edges with my fingers in order to split it open evenly. At first my fingers weren't long enough, but my father made me try until, after a while, he would hand me a fork and have me circle the muffin's outer perimeter with the tines, poking ever deeper until the muffin split in two. I'll never forget how good those muffins tasted. First we'd pop the halves under the broiler, face up, and leave them until golden brown. Then we'd spread them with copious quantities of butter and jam, and I was one kid who swore they tasted like cake!

Dad taught me little things like that, and I have taught them to my kids, too. English muffins are a safe and simple introduction to the use of an oven—provided, of course, that you're standing right there to snatch the children out of trouble if need be.

Still safer than oven cooking for kids, though, is one of Dad's old standbys. Wherever we went, he had an electric hot plate with him. Then, when we'd hit a town where a stove wasn't available, all he'd have to do was set it atop a rooming-house or dressing-room table or even a trunk, plug it in and start cooking.

Dad was always on the lookout for recipes that lent themselves to hot plate cooking or actors' chafing dish culinary artistry. There's one in particular—a Welsh rarebit—that is still very much a favorite with the Sterling family. A cook in some eastern Elks Club taught it to Dad, who taught it to me. I taught it to my daughters, and now they have added olives to the fixings. You'll find the recipe on page 166. Try it yourself and you'll see that it's nice, safe and so simple that even a child can prepare it. And yet it's a dish that you wouldn't hesitate to serve to guests—particularly if school's just let out and they're teen-agers.

A rarebit is made with cheese . . . which reminds me of another thing Dad stressed to me and which I now stress to you: If you want to get the most out of cheese, never eat it or serve it immediately after removing it from the refrigerator. Give it time to get up to room temperature. Cheese is like a living thing—it needs a chance to breathe. Its aroma needs time to get around. The smell is highly important to the flavor and enjoyment of just about anything you eat, but especially to cheese. When cheese is cold it has little or no character. But when you let it stand at room temperature for at least an hour before putting it into your mouth—well, all I can say is what Dad said to me: "Cheese tastes best when your nose knows it's coming!"

When I was old enough to be allowed into such places, he sometimes took me to saloons or men's clubs, and the crock of cheese on the bar was always the big attraction for me. Years later, when I was the ringmaster for "Big Top" on television, I had to journey to Philadelphia every week and I always stayed at the Warwick Hotel. One of my great delights was to go into its men's bar where a giant piece of aged cheddar was center stage at cocktail time. This, they told me, they always took out of the refrigerator well in advance of the daily onslaught of martini-and-cheese fanciers. Or, as the manager haughtily put it: "Sir, our motto is never to serve a cheese cold!"

There came a time in my youth that I can't look back upon with any particular relish. That was when vaudeville died, leaving Mother and Dad, and all of the other old-timers, with their world pulled out from under them. It wasn't a quick, painless death; it was long and lingering. Many factors contributed. First radio, then talking movies and then the final coup—the Depression. They were the chief deathblows, and each blow was more painful than the one before.

There were other contributing factors, some of them from within vaudeville itself, not from without. Factors that some show business people tried to cope with, to combat, but it was like trying to dam the Johnstown flood. The time was the Roaring Twenties, the Jazz Age, the Prohibition Era and—for those now seemingly prehistoric times—the country's morals were never worse. And vaudeville, as always, was a reflection of the times.

More and more of what we then called "blue dialogue" crept into the routines of many vaudeville acts, and nothing that people like Mother and Dad could do could stop it. They tried—many tried —but the more they tried, the worse it became. And vaudeville was the suicidal loser, for people stopped bringing the family.

Ironically, what was then considered "blue" or "risqué" would now be considered Sunday school stuff, if compared to some of today's television commercials and other commonplaces that every day invade our homes. Why, back in those days it was considered bold and brash, indecent and immoral, to wipe perspiration from under the arms, and theatre managers tried to keep such actions out of vaudeville routines. As for dialogue that included such lines as "that was when Fanny was still a girl's name" or "If Nature won't, Pluto will," those kinds of gags could earn a vaudevillian the hook in nothing flat. But what an I-don't-care actor could not get away with in one town, he could in another. And so, this along with radio, the talkies, the Depression and later on teevee caused vaudeville to die.

Mother and Dad had to find something else to do, so they opened a restaurant in, of all places, Ripon, Wisconsin—population last census: 6,163. Population then? Your guess is as good as mine, but keep it low. Why the folks picked Ripon I never did know. Maybe because the suffragette, Carrie Chapman Catt, was born there. Maybe because one of the founding meetings of the Republican Party was held there in 1854 and Dad was a Republican. Maybe because it is the home of Ripon College, and Mother and Dad wanted some of the knowledge to rub off on Betty and me. More realistically though, we were no doubt so short on dough we couldn't get to the next town.

We never did get to college, but Mother and Dad did open a restaurant, and its lack of success became almost legendary. Not because Ripon was small. Not because its people did not eat out very often. Not because ex-troupers would pass through and not have the price of a meal. But because Mother and Dad wouldn't be caught dead serving a commercial cut of meat when everyone knows that a choice cut tastes so much better.

However, though the restaurant was far from a commercial success, the parties that they gave at home for vaudeville friends who just happened to be dropping by in Ripon, Wisconsin—well, they'll always remain ripe in my memory. Mother and Dad would spread a buffet table—in the yard when the weather was right, in the parlor when the weather wasn't. Then they'd all sit around swapping show business stories, sipping their drinks and, most of all, shooting over to that buffet table like the game of Pitch Till You Win was just invented.

Cheeses of all sizes, shapes and forms always had a prominent place on that table. The rarebit, the spread, the chunks of Swiss and cheddar purchased at nearby farms. They all were there, but they were not alone in the limelight—there was the German Hot Potato Salad which tasted almost as good cold; baked ham, roast beef, baked beans, cole slaw and beefsteak tomatoes that Mother and Dad grew in their own little garden.

I still serve up all those delicacies, even the homegrown tomatoes, whenever Barbara and I have slack-and-sweater friends in. Try that German Hot Potato Salad recipe and you'll see why.

2

COOKING ON ONE BURNER

It was during the height or—if
you look at it that way—during the depth of Prohibition that
Mother and Dad took their fling at purveying cooked foods for a
price in Ripon. But food was not all that they purveyed.

The people of Wisconsin were then, as they are now, of rugged
stock, ready, able and in this case positively eager to rise to any
occasion. No matter what the setback, no matter what the catastro-
phe, no matter what the hardship inflicted upon them by Man or
Nature, with their own hands and hearts they pitched in to make
things right again.

Prohibition was one such crisis, but it was by no means a catas-
trophe. The farmers, a rugged breed, dug cellars under their barns,
installed vats and tubs and kilns, bent copper tubing this way and
that, fired up, tossed in much of their harvest be it fruit or be it
grain, and produced as good a grade of sipping whiskey as ever
bore a label. Their product bore no formal name, however. Some
called it Mother's Ruin, others called it Farmland Fog or the Spirits
of Wisconsin. But all agreed that there was none better to be had
in the land. And Heaven help the mobster who thought he might
horn in. This was hometown stuff, produced mainly to fulfill a need
and not to reap a profit, and any big-city hood who tried to take
over would ride out of town on the working end of a pitchfork.

It was in that setting, at that time, that Mother and Dad decided show business no longer was for them. So with the little money that they had they rented a little place across the road from the Green Lake Country Club a few miles outside Ripon. But it took some time to convince them before they settled down. Here's how it happened:

Circle stock was the folks' last meaningful fling at show business. And because circle stock was what brought us to Ripon, let me tell you about it. In the theatre, as you know, a stock company is basically a group of players "in residence" at a given theatre, usually presenting new plays every week. Therefore the one prime necessity of a stock company was to be located in a town or in a locale that could support it.

That's where Mother and Dad and circle stock came in. Dad formed a stock company in the Midwest, but he could find no community with enough daily potential patronage to keep it going. So he worked up a circuit of six towns, all of them close to one another, and his company presented their weekly plays not six nights a week in one town, but once a week in six different towns.

After the folks opened their restaurant, whoever happened to sleep, rehearse in the afternoon and then be off in the evening for another performance in another town.

That was circle stock. And Ripon was one of the towns on the Sexton Players Circuit. Along with Baraboo, Prairie du Chien, Wausau, Ladysmith and Beaver Dam. But in those dark, dwindling days of live theatre I guess nothing could keep it going. So Dad, stymied in his efforts to collect what it takes to keep alive at the box office—folding money—did what to him was the next best thing: he collected recipes.

Sauerbraten and Kartoffelklosse in Wausau. Wienerschnitzel in Baraboo. Duck in Orange Sauce in Prairie du Chien. Barbecued Spareribs in Beaver Dam. Grapefruit Pie and Cherry Pudding in Ladysmith. Hungarian Goulash in Ripon. You'll find all the recipes in this book just as Dad garnered them from many nice people, just as I garnered them from Dad, just as I use them now.

After the folks opened their restaurant, whoever happened to be passing through Ripon at just the right time could dig into whichever one of those dishes Dad felt like preparing on that particular day, at that particular hour. But most of the time, the daily fare was made up mainly of sandwiches and short-order dishes—

plus certain taboo liquids that never appeared on the menu. Customers had to ask for such refreshment, but they'd get it *only* if they had food along with it. Otherwise a guy, and maybe a girl, might get to feeling slightly light in the head, and Mother and Dad would have nothing to do with that kind of place.

Come to think of it, I guess that's why Art Stewart suggested, since they were convinced the time had come to swap the stage for a stove, that they settle in Ripon. Art was the owner-manager of the theatre there that the folks used as the base of operations for their circle stock company, and they got to be good friends. He was a member of the Green Lake Country Club, he knew of this place that was available nearby, and so, quicker than you can say ham-on-rye, the four of us were out there, cleaning, sweeping, polishing, getting ready for a bang-up opening.

And quite an opening it was. Art saw to it that practically every one of his country club cronies attended the premiere, and Mother and Dad saw to it that the food they ate would keep them always coming back for more.

Through all these years I still remember four of those opening-day dishes. In fact, every one of them have become standards around my house, especially the Green Lake Beefburger (page 121) which my daughters, The Sterling Sextet, and their friends say are "zing"—which translated into my-generation English means swell or scrumptious.

As for the Beefsteak Pie (pages 122–123), Ham and Sweet Potato Patties (pages 121–122) and Chicken Chili Casserole (page 136) that the folks premiered in Ripon, the girls merely classify them as zowie.

What was the Green Lake Beefburger? It was a glorified hamburger. All of the ingredients that went into it resulted from Dad's kitchen creativity, and the paying customers found it so delightfully different that they soon made it the specialty of the house.

Remember the word for it . . . zing! Not zowie.

I was approaching manhood in those days. I was fifteen and had an appetite to go with my age. I ate those Green Lake Beefburgers as if my right to vote depended upon it. Dad beamed with pride every time I went back for more, but he balked if I reached for a bottle of near beer. He didn't think I was that much of a man.

So, to prove him wrong, I wrote to an agent in Chicago and

offered my services as a leading man. Handsome, you know! I said I was nineteen, and I sent along a picture to prove it. A couple of months later, back came the reply. John D. Winninger, a big name in Midwest show business, wanted to interview me about becoming leading man in his stock company!

Dad let me go, let me get away with lying about my age, because he figured practical experience was better than what little education he could afford to give me. So I went to Wausau, Wisconsin, where Mr. Winninger was based, saw him, let him see me, got away with the lie, got the job, and I've been on my own ever since. And, you know, I wouldn't trade a minute of it.

Mother and Dad helped me pack my first trunk, putting this here, putting that there, and in one corner went their hot plate and nesting pans for cooking in hotels in towns where there were no boarding houses. It was Mother, forgetting that I was only fifteen (or maybe because I *was*), who insisted on the cooking utensils going along. I didn't want them. No sir, not me. I was going to eat out. I was going to be a man.

But, still, those nesting pans went along and they took up a minimum of space. Two of them together, serving as a double boiler, made a good substitute for a chafing dish. There was nothing that you couldn't cook if you put your mind to it. Provided, of course, that the hotel management permitted. Many hotels forbade cooking in rooms and no-cooking signs were everywhere. Nobody paid any attention to them, no matter how strongly—or how plaintively— they were worded. Some, very forceful, said "Positively No Cooking," and others, almost weeping, said "No Cooking, Please," and there even was one that combined the two:

PLEASE NO COOKING
POSITIVELY

But the sign that is most indelible in my memory read exactly like this:

ABSOLUTELY NO COOKING ALLOWED

———

POSITIVELY

———

ESPECIALLY CORNED BEEF AND CABBAGE

Now how could a guy ever forget a sign like that?

But still we cooked corned beef and cabbage. Not only in the hotel that displayed that sign, but everywhere else that we played whenever the spirit moved us. By "we" I mean whomever I happened to be rooming with at the time. Some of them were truly unforgettable characters. Such as the Australian ten years my senior who played the juvenile while I played the gray-bearded old men.

His two sisters came to America with him and became burlesque queens, and their mother, as soon as she heard, came after them to act as chaperone. His name was Stanley Davis. The last I heard he was general manager of a radio station in Indiana. He and his sisters and his mother could put together an East Indian curry that was hotter than anything in burlesque. Tastier, too. And surprisingly like the Waldorf-Astoria's shrimp curry recipe that you'll find on page 147. Try it and I think you'll agree it's a dish fit for a queen. And I don't mean a burlesque queen. And there was also the orchestra leader who'd tap his wife on the back of the neck with his fiddle if she missed her cue and, if that didn't work, with his wooden leg. Dick Wren was his name, and he was from Scotland. To illustrate not only the tenacity of the Scots but also the wonders that can be wrought with makeup, his artificial limb didn't prevent him from appearing all over the United States and Canada as one of the members of the Highland Kilties Band!

I had joined the Jack Kelly Tent Stock Company in Michigan the winter after the Winninger show closed, and that is when I met Dick. He was Kelly's music man and later when his wife, Ruby, joined the troupe, also did a couple of vaudeville numbers. Ruby was a lovely lady who not only could forgive those woodpecker knocks on the neck but also could cook and bake like a dream. Baking, as everyone knows, is an art that supposedly can't exist without a good oven. But Ruby not only showed that Scots are ingenious, but also demonstrated how show people could make do; she did her baking with nothing more than a griddle and a hot plate!

She did a lot of baking because kids like sweets, and everywhere that Dick and Ruby Wren went their son, Buddy, went too. Scones were Ruby's specialty, and her assortment seemed never-ending. Some had currants in them, some used mashed potatoes, while others were made with oatmeal. But my favorite scones were those

17

with raisins (recipe on page 191). As for Buddy, he must have thrived on them because today he's a successful dentist in, I think, Detroit.

Lloyd and Lola Connely were on the Kelly Tent Show circuit with us. Maybe it's nostalgia, but, looking back, I think they could make many, maybe most, of today's nightclub and television comedians look like a cake that had failed to rise. They had one routine in which they billed themselves as The Musical Chefs. The stage was set to look like a kitchen, and they'd come on dressed in white aprons and floppy chef's hats, walk up to a table loaded with bread and cake and doughnuts and hot dogs and ears of corn and I don't know what else and pick them up and pretend they were going to take a bite. But, instead, out would come music! Because all those goodies were phonies, made of plaster of Paris and camouflaging a wide variety of instruments. Harmonicas, kazoos, Jew's harps, flutes, clarinets, and, if I missed any wind instruments, those too. Maybe the idea came from the saw blades and files that people supposedly are always smuggling into prisons inside long loaves of bread. I don't know what triggered that act, but I do think that it helped to whet my appetite not only for eating but for cooking, too.

Off stage, Lola had a way with simple, no-cooking-needed dishes. I remember one, not only because it was a forerunner of today's packaged cottage cheese combinations, but also because the name she gave it was a play on the title of a then-popular comic strip, "The Toonerville Trolley." You'll find the recipe . . . and the title . . . on page 82.

Until now I haven't said much about them, but there were some unforgettable restaurants in some of the cities and the towns that we played. Restaurants to delight any food-loving, conversation-loving, atmosphere-loving stock player's heart. True, such places were few and far between. But once we had found them, we'd never forget them. And no matter what kind of food they served in this great melting pot of ours, they all had one thing in common —a proprietor who loved to cook, who loved cleanliness, and one who most of all loved people who loved good food.

I remember two of them in particular. One, in Kenosha, Wisconsin, was run by a German whose first name was Jake but whose last name I can't for the life of me remember. The other was a Greek whom I met many years later during my radio days in St.

Louis, Missouri. His name was Jim Mertikas, but we called him Mestika Jim. You'll find recipes of theirs throughout this book. Some I've named after these men, but even where I haven't, if the recipe is either Greek or German you can be sure that something of either Jim or Jake is a hidden ingredient.

Kenosha is a Lake Michigan port city that boasts not only Wisconsin's first public school but also a hearty breed of Americans descended from politically and religiously liberal Germans who fled the oppressions of their fatherland in the mid-1800s. Jake, who was a fairly recent arrival, was very much one of them. He was liberal, too, particularly in the size of his portions, the thickness of his accent and his guaranteed ability to give confounding answers to very simple questions. Jake's place was just on the outskirts of Kenosha, and Dad and Mother first introduced me to it. We'd go there for sauerbraten (you'll find Jake's recipe on page 101) every Saturday night that we were in the vicinity, and Dad would always ask Jake the same question: "How's business?" He always got the same answer: "If business is as bad next week as it was this week, I'm a son of a gun, that's all I hope."

Most German restaurants would serve sauerbraten with kartoffel-klosse (potato dumplings), but not Jake. Not that he couldn't make them or didn't approve of them, but purely because he thought his potato pancakes were more worthy companions. In fact, he was very adamant about it.

Anytime I or anyone else, in a purely frivolous moment of course, asked for sauerbraten and kartoffelklosse, Jake's reply would be: "With my sauerbraten goes only potato pancakes. If you do not like you don't eat!" You'll find the recipe for Jake's Potato Pancakes on pages 81–82. Try them—with or without sauerbraten—and *you'll* eat, too. Not only that, you'll like them or I'll be a son of a gun I'll bet!

Eating in Jake's place was never a hit-and-run affair. Jake's confounding pronouncements didn't make you want to hang around for more but, in any case, you had no choice, because he cooked virtually everything to order. Except the sauerbraten, of course, which he would begin on Tuesday in order to serve it on Saturday.

So Jake would suggest that we have some of his fish and chips to curb or maybe to whet our appetites while waiting. We knew Jake was joking. Jake knew Jake was joking. But we'd go along with the gag.

"Jake," we'd say, "fish and chips are a Scots and Limehouse-English dish, not a German dish. You wouldn't know what they looked like if you tripped over them. And, even if you did know how to make them, we wouldn't eat them because we came here for sauerbraten."

And Jake would reply: "My fish and chips are not for eating. They are for your appetite! Und they are German, I say!"

Then he'd produce an appetizer made of tomato herring and crumbled potato chips with sliced cucumber on the side. It sounds slightly oddball, I know, but taste it and I think you'll agree it's not oddball at all. But, please, don't call it "fish and chips." Call it "German Tomato Herring Spread," as I do for the recipe on page 57.

And, if and when you want some *real* fish and chips, you'll find an authentic recipe on page 159.

One thing that I would never want to do would be to match Jake's Wisconsin German cooking against Mestika Jim's Missouri Greek cooking. Both of them were masters of their art. Both of them, in their own native way of cooking, were unbeatable.

I met Jim in the early forties when I was first an announcer and later program director at radio station KMOX, known then as now as "The Voice of St. Louis." His restaurant was not far from our studios and it took me no time at all to discover it. He called it the Grecian Gardens and if you want to know on how much of a shoe-string Jim started, well, for the first few months he slept on a cot in the backroom.

Every talent that ever stopped in St. Louis got to know Jim Mertikas' place and it got so that after a while it seemed that everyone who lived in St. Louis did, too. It's said that the best way to tell a good ethnic restaurant from a bad one is by finding out the answer to the question: "Do the natives eat there?"

The answer in Mestika Jim's case was plain to see. Not only did Greeks eat there but two of them insisted that he move out of his backroom and in with them, maybe so he'd cook breakfast for them, too, his cooking was that good. They owned the American Theatre around the corner from the Grecian Gardens. They were brothers, household names in show business, George and Spyros Skouras, the makers of films with the 20th Century-Fox label. Obviously they not only knew movie talent, they also knew a good cook when they met one and they weren't about to let Mestika Jim out of their sight.

Since lamb is just about the Greek national dish, it wasn't surprising that Jim could do wonders with that much-maligned, mostly improperly cooked and therefore much-overlooked meat. When Jim cooked lamb, no matter what the cut, no matter what the method, it was sure to be a delicacy.

It's a safe bet that nine out of ten people who read this book are steak lovers. But I think that it's an equally safe bet that eight out of those nine never tasted lamb steak in their lives. Yet, believe me, lamb steak, properly done, can put many a beefsteak to shame.

Jim Mertikas had a way of broiling lamb steak that is guaranteed to make a lamb convert out of anyone who has ever eaten a beefsteak and asked for more. Jim would cut his lamb steaks from one-half inch to one inch thick and then marinate them for several hours (preferably overnight) in a mixture of lemon juice, oregano, olive oil and crushed garlic. How much of the marinade he used depended upon the thickness of the steaks and how many of them were to be marinated. Enough marinade to just cover is fine, but even less will do so long as the steaks are turned several times while marinating.

The only way Mestika Jim would broil them was over charcoal. He'd get his coals glowing hot, pat his steaks lightly with an absorbent, lint-free cloth towel to absorb most of the marinade, set them on a wire grill about four inches above the coals, brown one side and then the other. When they were almost done, he'd baste each side with the marinade. How long he cooked them depended upon the thickness of the steak and the customer's taste. Then he'd plop them on a hot platter, garnish them with mint leaves and shout for the waiter to pick 'em up. Jim would follow him out of the kitchen, big paw clutched around a bottle of red table wine from the wine presses of Naoussa, Greece, and shout for the waiter to bring glasses all around. If that combination doesn't make you want to try lamb steak, Mestika Jim style, then you must be both a vegetarian and a member of the WCTU.

Speaking of how Jim Mertikas marinated steaks reminded me that he wasn't by any means the only one who did so, except of course that the others marinated beef rather than lamb. Take Jake back there in Kenosha. He'd choose a lowly boneless chuck steak, marinate it in beer for several hours and then plunk it under the broiler soaking wet. Twenty minutes later you'd think you were eating porterhouse!

I must have encountered a hundred different ways of marinating steaks in my travels, and you'll find a few of them on pages 91–92.

But to get back to Jim. He had a way with vegetables, cooked or in salads, with chicken, with lamb, with fish, with macaroni, even with T-bone steaks, and you'll find many of his recipes in this book.

Take celery. If ever there has been a neglected vegetable, this is it. It can be used in many ways other than chopped in salads, boiled in soups, stuffed with cheese or in company with a dish of radishes, olives and scallions. Mestika Jim's recipe for braised celery is unusual enough to prove it. Although it hardly can be called a Greek dish, it is his creation and it is a delight. Try the recipe on page 84 and see for yourself.

Yes, it was a good life for a boy still in his teens, meeting good people, eating good food, making good money . . . $60 or $70 a week was good money in those days. I was barnstorming the West all the way from the Mississippi to the Pacific with occasional forays into Canada, playing Mr. Kelly one season, playing Mr. Cohen the next, getting the kind of experience that no actor can possibly get today. I was happy as can be, sure that I was on the glory road to Broadway.

But not even such hit plays of the times as *The Cohens and the Kellys* could keep pulling them in. When the Winninger show closed I joined the Jack Kelly show. Next it was the Robeson Players, and after that the Norma Ginnivan Stock Company. We brought good theatre to just about every town and city big enough to have street lights in Wisconsin, Minnesota, Illinois, Michigan, Iowa, Missouri, Indiana and Ohio.

I played the lead in some of the greatest melodramas and musicals of the times, *Jerry for Short, Shepherd of the Hills,* and *Smilin' Through*, to name just a few. And between the acts every one of us had a vaudeville specialty to keep the customers happy. (Mine was song and dance.) But not even these diversions could keep the people coming.

With the stock companies fast disappearing, the next stop was the Circus Revue in a really wonderful olio that we called "Circus Days" and that took us through the Far West, up and down the

West Coast and into Canada's distant provinces. I remember two things best about that tour: how I suddenly found myself playing the drums one day in Seattle when our drummer showed up drunk, and a recipe for Potatoes Au Gratin that I scrounged from a little hash joint I wandered into on Geary Street in San Francisco. This little six-stool place served the potatoes with steak. The steak was very ordinary—but the potatoes. . . . I gave the counterman a ticket for the show and he gave me the recipe. I pass it on to you on pages 84–85.

Nothing could save live theatre, though. Certainly not me, a teen-age kid playing old-man leads, not me doing a song-and-dance between the acts, not me playing the drums, not me giving away tickets in exchange for recipes. Nothing could save us because there is a fundamental law about depressions: When people don't have money, they don't spend.

My agent, who had to eat too, began to book me into nightclubs and speakeasies. The pay was good—better than stock—but I didn't like a minute of it. The owners were mainly hoods, the audiences were mainly drunks and courtesy was mainly nil.

So when the WPA set up the Federal Theater and an old family friend phoned to offer me the juvenile lead in *Lightnin'* I didn't hesitate a second in saying yes. Not even when I told the manager of the 5100 Club, a Chicago night spot where I was then working.

"Whaddaya mean you're quitting an 80-buck-a-week job to work for 94 skins a month? Whatcha going to do? Go to work for those mugs down the street?"

I assured him I was not, definitely was not, going to work for a rival mob. Visions of how the gang had cut up Joe E. Lewis danced in my head. I guaranteed him I was not. So he let me go, and a week later the emcee that replaced me was killed at the microphone when caught in the crossfire between two mugs shooting it out! Danny Thomas replaced him and he was lucky. He survived, as his television fans know.

Those were happy days in the Federal Theater, especially when we stopped touring and settled down to what was called "production stock" in Peoria, Illinois. Two people made me particularly happy . . . the guy who played the 82-year-old Lightnin' Bill Jones and the orchestra's first violinist.

The first gent, Guy Beach, took off and didn't come back. So I, a teen-ager, stepped into the part that the unforgettable Frank Bacon had made famous for years on Broadway.

And the first violinist in the WPA orchestra—ah, I'll never forget him either! His name was Ned Pechairno, and the things that he could do for spaghetti sauce and a host of other Italian delicacies could, I'm sure, fill a book. You'll find several pages of his outstanding recipes in later chapters. Ned had an apartment in Peoria complete with stove, icebox and ingredients by the score. Two or three times a month he'd have a bunch of us over for an evening of unforgettable food, fiddle and festivities.

I don't know the Italian name for smorgasbord, or even if there is one, but I do know that Ned set the best. Five dishes in particular have become very much a part of the Sterling family entertainment, and I suggest that you give each of them a whirl in your house, too. You'll find all of them in the recipe section of this book . . . Anchovies on Toast, Shrimp and Mushroom Mix, Baked Clams, Peppers with Anchovy Sauce and Marinated Mushrooms. Make sure, though, to prepare enough so that everyone can go back for seconds and thirds and maybe even fourths.

Yes, those were happy days. But, like everything else, even the Federal Theater had to come to an end. And when it did it was back to the nightclubs for me. I was booked into a Peoria nitery as emcee and, though I naturally didn't know it, that was the turning point of my career, my life.

A man invited me over to his table one night, introduced himself as Howard Dorsey, said he was an announcer on Peoria's Radio Station WMBD, and asked if I'd like to be part of a one-shot, hour-long variety show they had in the works. All they wanted from me was twelve minutes of songs and gags, and in exchange they'd pay me all of five dollars. I jumped at the offer. Not at the money, but at the chance of trying out a new medium—radio.

Well, I tried it and I liked it and the radio audience liked me. The next thing I knew I was working full time for WMBD as announcer, actor, producer of dramatic shows and second banana on the station's Saturday night barn dance.

That job led to other jobs in radio. I was program director at WBBM, the CBS outlet in Chicago, when the big break came. Arthur Godfrey was leaving his early-morning show at WCBS, New York, and they were looking for someone to replace him. I shot off an audition record. They called me and I got the job, which I held for eighteen years before transferring to an even happier home at WHN, the pillar of Park Avenue radio. Now here am I sitting high on a Connecticut hill, master of all I survey, except of course Barbara and our six daughters.

3

GO EAST, YOUNG MAN, GO EAST . . .

I arrived in New York, the Big Apple, to broadcast my new show for the first time on November 1, 1948. That week the whole nation went to the polls, not to vote to see if I should stay but to choose either Harry Truman or Thomas Dewey as the next President of the United States.

Both Mr. Truman and Jack Sterling were the winners. I left my hotel room, wandered into a saloon (they're not called that anymore and for the life of me I don't know why) near the CBS studios and settled down to hear the election returns over a drink or two and a midnight supper. I was already savoring the good food of fine New York restaurants.

I was digging into a shrimp cocktail (you'll find a good basic sauce recipe for one on page 148), and my eyes had just become adjusted to the light. There, seated at a table on the opposite side of the room, was a man whose footsteps I'd always wanted to follow. I grabbed a pencil and piece of paper and scribbled a note: "Can one John D. Winninger leading man buy another a drink?"

The waiter took it over. The man read it, let out a whoop, stood up and waved. I grabbed my drink and double-timed to his table. We shook hands and sat down, and Ralph Bellamy and I have been good friends ever since. In fact, he also was a lifesaver or, more like it, a show-saver.

I told him what I was doing, that I was scared to death, that I wanted guests on my early morning show but still didn't know where to find them. And the words he said to me meant, "Kid, your worries are over." And they were, because with Ralph Bellamy as a talent scout I couldn't miss. Ralph himself was the first guest I ever had and then, almost one on top of the other, came Gene Autry, the immortal Bobby Clark, Jimmy Durante, Louis Armstrong, Jack Benny, Lionel Hampton, Red Skelton . . . you name them, the chances are they were in the studio with me at 6 or 7 in the morning (usually before they went home and went to bed) at one time or another.

Bellamy was starring in the Broadway hit *State of the Union* at the time. He proposed me for membership in the Lambs Club, with Gene Autry and Bobby Clark as my seconders. The club soon taught me something that I guess I had known all of my life: The food that theatrical people like to eat isn't much different from the food in all of the theatrical boarding houses throughout the country. The menu at the Lambs reads like a collection of all of the dishes ever served by every Mrs. Murphy show folk ever knew—even when her name was Mrs. Haggerschmidt, Mrs. Goldberg or Mrs. Von der Heuvel. The several Lambs Club standby recipes that you'll find in this book will show you what I mean: Chicken Gumbo Soup, German Apple Pancake, Chicken in the Pot, Irish Lamb Stew, Veal Shank. Dishes like that. Simple, every day, good. Just as good as the things that go on there in the Lambs while an actor is having his dinner. Oh, the gags, the jokes, the belly laughs, that you'll hear there!

Harry Hershfield, one of the master storytellers of all time, delights in spinning Lambs Club yarns. Like the saga of the Lambs' Number One trencherman, Kelsey Allen, one of New York's foremost drama critics of days gone by. He was a roly-poly if ever there was one, and under constant pressure from his doctor to shed weight.

Kelsey was having lunch one day in the Lambs' grill room and his table was inundated by enough food—all very heavy food—to stoke the fires of not one man but three. Senator Ford . . . Edward Hastings Ford, showman, raconteur, very funny man of stage, screen, radio and television fame . . . chanced by and, most reprovingly, said, "Kelsey, you're supposed to be on a diet!"

"Oh yes," Kelsey replied. "Thanks for reminding me." And then he turned and shouted: "Waiter, bring me my crackers and milk!"

Senator Ford was always quick on the uptake, too. I made the mistake of asking him one day how he came by his middle name, Hastings. He explained: "I was named after a battle. Not, however, the battle in which William the Conqueror fought in 1066. My mother won this one from my father."

Another great Lambs Club storyteller is Walter Kinsella, a professional's professional who has been cast in just about every conceivable role in every facet of show business from silent movies to Broadway stage shows, and probably 9,000 radio and television shows! Walter tells the story of Brian Foy, one of the Seven Little Foys, calling an employment agency in quest of a new cook.

"We have just the woman for you," the agency man said. "At one time she was one of the finest cooks in the land. But, you might say, she's been in retirement for the past few years. Now, however, she is ready to resume where she left off." And he reeled off an impressive list of past positions.

"Sounds marvelous," said Brian Foy, "but how come she hasn't worked in years?"

"Well, if you must know, she was in prison and she just got out."

"In prison! For heaven's sake, what for?"

"Murder," said the agency man. "She poisoned her husband. But I assure you, she's a wonderful cook, a truly marvelous cook."

"You convinced me," said Brian Foy. "She's a wonderful cook and I'd hire her in a minute, except for one thing. . . ."

"What's that?" asked the agency man.

"If only she'd shot her husband, not poisoned him!"

The teller of that tale of a cook with the wrong ingredients, is no slouch as a cook himself. Walter lives at the Lambs now, but he once had an apartment on Park Avenue where he often entertained show business friends. He fondly recalls one time that several cronies, including Bert Wheeler of Wheeler and Woolsey renown, were coming in for a libation and then, while dinner was cooking, they would cab to the old Polo Grounds to watch the old New York Giants do battle with the old Brooklyn Dodgers.

Walter had an electric rotisserie for occasions like that, and for cooking while doing a Broadway show. Just place a chunk of meat or a bird on the spit, put the shield back in place, flip a switch and take off for wherever he was going. And when he returned the meat was done just right . . . provided, of course, the cooking time and the be-away-from-home time coincided.

"Bert hated lamb but loved veal," Walter said, "and so I called my butcher and ordered a leg of veal sent over. He delivered a leg of lamb instead, and I didn't discover the error until too late. There was nothing for me to do but try to bluff my way through.

"So I set the heat on low, figuring we would be gone about three hours. But the game went into extra innings and it was more than five hours before we got back. That was my lucky break. The lamb was cooked white. So I served it, and Bert tasted it, loved it, had two more helpings. Then, sated and satisfied, he leaned back and said 'That's the best veal I ever ate in my life!'"

Harry Hershfield, like Bert Wheeler, is a veal lover. He was in Manhattan's famed Stage Delicatessen enjoying a veal shank (you'll find a recipe on pages 94–95) when a piece of unforgettable byplay and repartee took place, as it always does when anyone dares take on Max Asnass, the Stage's ebullient proprietor.

"A customer came in," Harry recalled, "and put his expensive homburg on the narrow shelf that passes for a hat rack. The homburg fell off and into the mustard on one of the tables. 'Max,' the customer screamed, 'look what happened. This is a very expensive hat.' To which Max replied: 'So what? This is very expensive mustard!'"

And so, on pages 124–125 you'll find a recipe for roast leg of veal, coated with very expensive mustard, that I dedicate to Harry Hershfield, Bert Wheeler, Walter Kinsella and Max Asnass.

As for the inimitable Senator Ford, you'll find a recipe for chicken-beef-noodle soup on pages 85–86 dedicated to him in payment for the following saga: "I went into a very dubious-type restaurant in a strange town for dinner one night and ordered soup. When it came something was swimming around in it. I called the waiter over and asked: 'What's this in my soup?' He studied it from every angle, then said, 'I'll have to call the boss, I don't know one insect from another!'"

New York, I soon found out, has what I consider some of the finest restaurants to be found anywhere in the world. One such place was Louis and Armand's, which was once but is no longer located (and that is a pity) on 52d Street between Madison and

Park Avenue. I guess I might say that it was practically my second home when I first came to New York.

Nor was I the only one who was attracted to the place. Ed Murrow, Walter Cronkite, Ed Sullivan, John Cameron Swayze, Bill Downs, David Schoenbrun and any number of CBS overseas correspondents also preferred the intimacy of Louis and Armand's to a hotel room or an apartment with paper-thin walls. Why, even Chet Huntley of NBC ate and passed the time of day there.

Victor . . . I never heard his last name and sometimes I doubt that he had one . . . was the maître d', and when he got into the cooking act everyone there knew they were in for a special treat. Louis and Armand specialized in many fine Italian and French delicacies of which they were justifiably proud. Dishes with exotic names. But, because of my hours, the one that I ordered most often was a basic American breakfast food, ham and eggs, but done as too few Americans have ever tasted them.

I went off the air, then as now, at 10 o'clock in the morning. Time for breakfast. And I'd be hungry. I'd hasten through whatever studio chores needed doing and then, if I hadn't been saddled by our sales department with a luncheon date with a sponsor, I'd hasten over to Louis and Armand's to order Eggs Benedict . . . wonderfully fancied-up ham and eggs as only Louis and Armand and their chef could prepare them. The recipe is on pages 167–168. Try it. I'm sure you'll like it.

But before I get carried away, let me tell you about Barbara, my wonderful wife Barbara.

It was during my fourth year at WCBS that I met her. The first time I'd seen her, though, was long before that when she went to work as a second secretary for Margaret Arnold, whose offices were down the hall from mine. I thought Barbara was an extremely attractive young lady and quite competent, too. So when my secretary left to get married, I asked Margaret if her second secretary could become my one and only secretary.

Margaret agreed, and that was my introduction to Miss Barbara MacGregor, now Mrs. Jack Sterling.

Until then there had been nothing more than an occasional hello or goodbye when I quit work for the day at the ripe old hour of 10 (A.M.) and we happened to pass in the corridor. That's the way it was for the next four months or so, too: purely an employer-employee relationship. Then Barbara told me that her parents were moving to Washington and she was going to take a teaching job there so she could be with them.

She was, she explained, a graduate of Marymount College in Tarrytown, New York, with a teacher's degree, and she had been offered a position with newly opened Marymount College in Arlington, Virginia.

She'd been a delightful gal, a perfect secretary, and I'd taken some notice of her but not too much really. So purely as a gesture, a way of thanking someone who had been loyal, capable, I invited her to have lunch with me at Giovanni's, a very fine restaurant in the fifties.

Each of us, I remember, ordered a clam aspic salad, but for the life of me I can't remember even trying to figure out what all went into it because that's when it all started. That was my first real introduction to the young lady who later became my wife and the mother of my six lovely little girls. That luncheon was the first time, really, that I'd ever had the opportunity to just sit down and talk with her, and it began to dawn on me that I was about to lose a precious thing. So I know you'll understand why I never did ask Giovanni for the clam aspic recipe. But you will find one on page 161 that I'm sure is quite like it.

Then came the courtship. Barbara went to Washington to be with her Mother and Dad, and my crazy early morning schedule made seeing each other a constant problem in logistics. But we got a break in the summer, again because of circumstance.

Her family had a summer home in Spring Lake, a nice resort community on the New Jersey shore, and I started to do Big Top. You may remember it. A circus show with me as the Ringmaster on television every Saturday morning. It came out of Philadelphia, which meant that I'd prerecord my Saturday morning radio show in New York, do my Friday morning show live and then hotfoot it for the Pennsylvania Railroad Station and a fast train to Philadelphia for rehearsal.

Came the summer and an invitation from Barbara's folks to weekend with them at Spring Lake, which is roughly midway between New York and Philadelphia, but on the coast, of course, and not inland. So instead of taking a train to Phillie, I'd drive down, do Big Top, get back to Spring Lake about 3 o'clock Saturday afternoon and spend a very pleasant, though hectic weekend with Barbara and her family and assorted other guests.

Barbara's mother could work wonders with salads, perfect summertime fare. She was especially good at fixing salads made with seafoods, since the ingredients were only a few yards away—yours for the casting and catching. Try Mother MacGregor's Fresh-Caught Seafood Salad recipe on page 76.

Yes, they were pleasant weekends there in Spring Lake. So pleasant, in fact, that not even getting up at 2 A.M. Monday in order to be back on the New York radio air at 6 could put a damper on them.

That was our courtship, and it was punctuated by marriage in St. Catherine's Church in Spring Lake on June 20, 1953—undoubtedly the hottest June 20th the Jersey shore had ever known. We thought even the wedding cake was going to wilt. It didn't though . . . probably it was all the eggs in it that held it together. We all survived (the heat, I mean, not the wedding cake; that was delicious) possibly because of the delightfully cool champagne punch (recipe on page 193).

Barbara and I went to Bermuda on our honeymoon. I think it was the first place I'd ever been where I didn't spend a lot of my time gathering recipes. There were many places there, all the way from Somerset to St. David's, where the food was amazingly delightful and someday, I swear, I'm going to go back and collect all the recipes.

After our honeymoon we stayed at the Westchester Country Club until our apartment in mid-Manhattan was ready. And there, horrors, I learned that my bride could not cook! But it took weeks for me to find out, because the first dinner I ate in our first home, and every one that Barbara supposedly prepared thereafter, tasted as if it had come straight from the Waldorf.

Let me tell you about that first-day dinner.

I didn't get home until late because of a lot of chores that needed doing at the studio after I'd gone off the air. So it was that I didn't walk in the door until dinner was ready to be put on the table. And what a dinner it was! Marvelous! Nothing ritzy, nothing fancy, but still a dinner that had lots of class, lots of originality. Just pancakes stuffed with meat—but good, very very good. And strangely remindful of my good Greek friend of St. Louis days, Jim Mertikas.

33

In fact, I remarked upon it to Barbara while congratulating her, the chef, for the fine cuisine. She smiled a lovely, but secretive, smile.

From that day on I'd often come home to find the janitor, a nice old Greek gentleman named Parris, strangely puttering around the place. I never knew that we had so many curtain rods, shower rods, window shades and this and that and the other thing that needed adjusting. So always Mr. Parris was there to adjust them. And always dinner was good. And always dinner was strangely remindful of Jim Mertikas.

Then, weeks later, when Barbara felt secure enough around a stove to confess, she told me that Mr. Parris had been teaching her how to cook. And that first-dinner recipe was his. Try it, and who knows? Maybe you'll want to go off on a second honeymoon. It's the Stuffed Pancake recipe on page 123. The many steps involved make it appear to be an involved creation, but really it's quite simple. And very tasty.

Once Barbara and I got settled down to married life—some people would say "once the honeymoon was over," but as far as the two of us are concerned, that day will never come—I discovered for what seemed to be the first time in my life just how wonderful it was to have a stay-put home. You may be sure that I made the most of it, and I do not mean the slippers-and-pipe routine. Sure, I had my share of that, too, but here I was at long last able to have friends in for something other than what could be cooked on one burner.

We entertained whenever my silly hours would permit, sometimes for dinner, sometimes for lunch, but most often just for cocktails, conversation and canapés . . . the latter courtesy of Mr. Parris, who introduced me to a whole new world of Greek-style appetizers.

Mr. Parris worked wonders with the commonplace. For example, bacon. He'd nip off small pieces, wrap them around chicken livers, shrimp, crabmeat, stuffed olives, sweet pickles or lemon-spiked scallops or anchovies or clams or oysters or artichoke hearts or whatever struck his fancy, shove them under the broiler and, presto, out would come food for the gods. Being Greek, Mr. Parris used lemon juice for just about everything, even things that had little or nothing to do with flavoring a recipe. Here are some of the tricks that he taught me:

1. Add a small amount of lemon juice to the water while boiling fish in order to make the flesh firm and white.

2. Add a few drops of lemon juice or vinegar to the water to hold eggs together while poaching.

3. To get the most juice possible out of a lemon, heat it before squeezing.

4. Add a tablespoon of lemon juice or vinegar to the water to eliminate the odor of cooking cabbage.

5. When only a small amount of lemon juice is needed, puncture the skin with a fork and squeeze it through the holes.

6. One teaspoon of lemon juice to every quart of water will make rice lighter and fluffier.

7. Rub hands with a slice of lemon to remove vegetable stains.

8. To whip cream more easily, add a few drops of lemon juice and chill before starting to beat it.

That was our Mr. Parris. I wouldn't be surprised if he used lemon juice to oil squeaky hinges!

So went our marriage, and a little more than a year later along came Patty Ann, our first child. We had room enough in our apartment, even with Mr. Parris puttering around. But when we knew that Bethy was on the way we decided it was time to stop being cliff-dwellers, get out of New York and put our roots down somewhere. We searched Long Island, New Jersey and Westchester, but finally decided on New Canaan, Connecticut. And here we are.

THE FOODS OF NEW YORK

Until now about all I've talked about is what living and collecting recipes was like during a lifetime in show business. Now, looking back on all those happy, memorable years, I'd say that I have just one regret . . . I never did get cast in a play on Broadway. And like everyone else who ever set foot on a stage, this was my ambition. Even more, I might add, it was my folks' hope for me, too.

But I did get to ride down Broadway as the Big Top Ringmaster in Macy's Thanksgiving Day Parade. And every inch of the way, with the kids laughing for the guy that they saw on TV and the grownups cheering for the gent that they heard on radio, I thought of Mother and Dad. I thought how happy they must be to see me on Broadway, looking down upon me from wherever it is that good show people go when life is over.

I thought, too, what irony it was that I, in just one hour, in just one episode of one nationally televised show, played to a larger audience than Mother and Dad did in their lifetime of trouping from state to state, town to town, theatre to theatre. Joining The Lambs, the mecca of showmen, was in a sense making good on one of Dad's unrealized ambitions. And so I think, yes, life has changed, show business has changed, I have changed as all the others of us who grew up in a taylor trunk have changed. And I

count my blessings on having made it big in the medium of radio
—a medium I don't think had even been invented when my folks
took their first curtain call.

Things have changed so much that today I live in a house bigger,
and certainly far nicer, than many of the theatrical boarding houses
in which we stayed. That's from necessity, though. The bigness, I
mean. When there are six children in the family . . . well, you see
the need.

Things have changed so much, too, that today I do my recipe
collecting in the most fertile gustatory terrain known to man . . .
the Canyons of Manhattan, lined on all sides by some of the finest
restaurants in the world. When I say fine, I don't mean fancy—I
don't mean lace curtains or outlandish prices. I mean the food is
fine, no matter what the decor, no matter what the tab.

Like all who toil in mid-Manhattan, I have the foods of all nations
at my toe tips . . . within easy walking distance of the WHN
studios on Park Avenue and 54th Street. Is my mood for Italian
cuisine? I know of no better place than the Rose Restaurant, just a
couple of doors from Toots Shor's (no slouch of a restaurant either)
on 52d Street.

The Rose, or Rose's as it's most commonly called, is one of those
increasingly rare restaurants. It's family owned and family operated;
and the family intends to keep it that way for at least one more
generation to come. The first generation is Mama Rose and Papa
Gigi Buzzalino. Mama can be found out in front every day, while
Papa holds forth in the kitchen, turning out culinary gems that only
a master can create. But then, why not? After all, Gigi will never
see 79 again and so he's had lots of practice. Try his Lobster Americano recipe on page 162 and you'll see what I mean.

Son Angelo, "Buzzy" to everyone, is the second generation, and
there's nothing that Mama and Papa can do that he can't do. And
perhaps there's one thing that he can do much better: see to it that
bartenders Tony, Frank, Ralph and Walter fill the glasses to the
brim when a customer orders a drink.

The third generation hasn't stepped into the picture yet. He is
Paul the Second (Grandpa Gigi is Paul the First) and he is cur-
rently majoring in business administration at the University of
Toledo with, you can be sure, courses in restaurant management
very much a must.

The menu at Rose's reads much like a menu in any Italian restaurant. But when the food you've ordered is set before you and you take the first tentative taste, you know that this is what sets Rose's place apart. And like all Italian restaurants, many of Gigi's specialties do not appear on the menu, probably because there just isn't room enough for them all. So the thing to do is to evince curiosity. Ask a waiter or ask Buzzy or ask Mama Rose and they'll suggest Gigi originals by the score. The Lobster Americano is one of them. But no matter what you order, the price is right. Not cheap, not expensive—in between.

When I really want to splurge, I take Barbara to the "21" Club. Bob Kriendler, Pete, Mr. Mack and all the rest of the wonderful people there have been very nice to me through the years, and "21" food has been even nicer. I have sampled many great dishes there and then talked about them many times on the air.

You'll find three of them in the recipe section. One is fine dinner fare . . . Faisan à la Choucroute. Another is fine breakfast fare, but created by Chef Anthony Pedrette for any meal of the day, especially for after-the-theatre supper. And a third is nothing more than the lowly hamburger. But when you taste Hamburger "21" it's not lowly any more.

In the Chinese food department—at least for my tastes—I must call Bill Chan's New Gold Coin Restaurant one of the very best. When I visit Bill's tastefully decorated jade palace it is like being in a restaurant all my own. I have the run of the place, including the kitchen, which most chefs hold inviolate. In fact, I'm so welcome there that Bill and his chef, Richard Yee, have even fitted me out with a chef's cap all my own. You'll see a picture of Bill and Richard and me elsewhere in this book, and if you want to know that translation of the Chinese words on my cap, well, in all modesty I must tell you that it's this: "The world's greatest chef!"

I'm very proud to be able to say that any time I've ever sent people to the New Gold Coin, Bill or his able aides Tommy and Roy have never failed to roll out the welcome mat—and, most important of all, great Chinese food. You'll find many Chinese recipes in this book. Not all of them are identified as coming from Bill Chan's place, but you can be sure that just about all have something of the New Gold Coin touch.

There is one gathering place that cannot possibly be bypassed in any rundown of eateries in New York, The Culinary Capital of the Continent. And that is Toots Shor's palace of platitudes, famed the world over not so much for its food as for its proprietor. But I assure you, the food and drink are excellent too.

Toots has been a friend of mine almost from the moment I arrived in New York. And of all the stories about food that he has ever told me, perhaps the best one concerns a reporter who once interviewed him about cuisine à la Toots Shor.

"Mr. Shor," the reporter asked, "what is your favorite type of food?" Toots replied, "American food, good plain American food." Then he went on to extol the qualities of the good plain American food to be had in his sportsman's hangout . . . beef stew, rare roast beef, corned beef hash. Toots described the marvels of each, done the Toots Shor way, in wonderful detail. The reporter took it all down, drooling with Toots about the wonders of good plain American food. When Toots was done singing their virtues, he asked one more question, "Mr. Shor, what is your favorite American dish?" And Toots, face straight as a die, replied, "Veal piccata"!

Toots is the eternal practical joker and the best proof of that statement is the three Toots Shor recipes in this book. I asked Toots to favor me with his good plain American formulas for beef stew, rare roast beef and corned beef hash because I've tried them all and they are good.

So what did he send me? A note that read: "Dear Jack, Here are the three recipes you asked for." Enclosed were recipes for Potted Chicken (Jewish), Shrimp Scampi (Italian), and Hungarian Goulash!

A great deal of my luncheon time is spent with our sales people at WHN, our clients and their advertising agency representatives. In short, several hours a week at noon I am sure to be caught in the Madison Avenue rush—the Mad Ave maelstrom.

While I enjoy this kind of companionship, while I wouldn't be where I am today without it, the fact remains that it is a form of work and that it comes after four taxing hours at a microphone. So there are times when I feel that I must escape. When one of those moments hits me, one of my favorite hideaways is a Japanese restaurant, the Saito, on 52d Street. There I can sit all alone in a corner and just think, think, think while the lovely little waitress putters around, preparing the food on an electric plate built into the table which, in true Japanese fashion, is only about a foot high.

The Saito is a fine place to take the family for a dinner that's different. A fond memory in my house is the first time Barbara and I took the Six Sterling Sisters there and we all sat cross-legged around the little Japanese tables as Miss Ruth—I guess you'd call her the Saito's public relations gal—explained the intricacies of Oriental cooking, Japanese style. It was like being in a doll house.

Two of my favorite Saito dishes are Beef Sukiyaki and Mizutaki, a chicken creation. Miss Ruth was good enough to permit me to include their recipes in this book (pages 126 and 140) and I'm appreciative, as I am sure you will be after trying them.

In the photograph section of this book you'll find Ed Sullivan and me in one of New York's newer restaurants, Umberto's, on 53d Street between Fifth and Madison avenues. The man in the photo with us, in case you can't guess, is Umberto.

I could go on naming great New York restaurants forever, it seems. Unfortunately, however, there isn't room enough to review them all or to include their recipes. So I'll leave the restaurant-hopping and recipe collecting to you. Just search around a bit and you're sure to come up with favorites of your own.

I've made, as you have gathered by now, many friends, people whom I would not otherwise have even met had I not found my niche in New York radio. Especially musical people, of whom there were so many. Louis Armstrong, Cab Calloway, Steve Lawrence and Eydie Gorme, Patti Page (she's a sensational singer with a sensational yen for pumpkin pie, by the way), to name just a few.

Frank Chacksfield, the great English orchestra leader, has become one of my dearest acquaintances. The first time we met was when his song, "Ebb Tide," was so popular. He came to New York on a personal appearance tour, and I had him as a guest on my WCBS show. He made me promise to look him up if ever I was in London and when I made the hop a few years later on a BOAC press flight, my two main companions and guides were Charles Collingwood, the CBS correspondent there, and Frank "Ebb Tide" Chacksfield. Charlie introduced me to a broadcasting studio that made me feel very much a part of contemporary history, and Frank introduced me to Panniers, a marvelous restaurant in London.

What an introductory meal we had in Panniers! We opened with an avocado pear stuffed with boiled baby prawns (very small shrimp), with just a touch of a very light French dressing. That, I think, was the best seafood cocktail I've ever eaten. It was followed by Duck à l'Orange—duck with orange sauce—and it was superb. Yet, in tasting it, I had the surprise of my life because it did not taste much different from the theatrical boarding house recipe that is included in this book on page 133.

My program was broadcast live from London during my all-too-brief stay there, and Charlie Collingwood was good enough to accompany me to the studio. He took me deep underground, into what appeared to be a bomb shelter, then stood back while I looked about in amazement.

"You must be kidding. A studio down here?" I asked.

And Charles Collingwood replied: "Not just any studio. *The* studio. *The* studio from which Ed Murrow broadcast during World War Two, opening with those unforgettable words . . . 'This is London.'"

Experiences like that I can never forget. And there are many other unforgettable things. Like the morning when I was on the air and one of the boys from the newsroom came in and said there was a phone call for me. I reminded him that I never take phone calls while on the air, and he told me that I'd want to take this one and besides I'd have a six or seven minute break in thirty seconds because Ken Banghart would be on with the 7:30 newscast. So I said "Okay, who is it?" and he said "Never mind, you'll find out."

And find out I did. When I got to the phone the most unmistakable voice I've ever heard, except perhaps Jimmy Durante's, came trumpeting over the line: "Hey, Pops, how goes it?" And then, as though I didn't recognize gravel when I heard it, superfluously added, "This is Satch."

With him, he said, was my long-time friend and associate in the Sterling Quintet, Tyree Glenn. They'd been driving back from an appearance in Washington and had been listening to me on the car radio. They had heard me talk about cooking (as I so often do), and now that they were safely ensconced in his apartment, would I like to come up when I got off the air and join them in a pot of Creole Red Beans and Rice?

Would I???? I was off the air at 10 and I think I was digging into that Louisiana delicacy at 10:02.

Several years later, Satch and Patti Page and I did a Christmas

42

show together at the Waldorf-Astoria. When we were done, Louis said to me, "Gee, Pops, I haven't got a Christmas present for you" and I said "Oh yes you have. Just give me that recipe for the beans and rice that we had at your place five or ten years ago!" Louis did, and you'll find it on page 88. If it makes you smile like Louis' famous smile, then this book and I have done our job.

And while I'm in a happily smiling mood, let me introduce my daughters because they are, I guess, what I have most to smile about. So here they are, one by one, in order of appearance . . . The Sparkling, the Scintillating, the Sensational Sterling Sisters!

Patty Ann, Patricia Ann, is the oldest. She is fourteen and doing her level best to be the typical teen-ager. In the past few months however, we have been able to tone down her hairdo a little bit. Hairdos are typical of the growing pains that Patty is undergoing at the moment. She's really a wonderful girl, a very pretty girl, a good dancer, quite quiet when she wants to be, very flamboyant at other times, and signs of a good brain are cropping out here and there.

Patty makes me wonder, though, about my decision to put in a second telephone . . . known in my house (as in yours probably) as "the children's phone." Patty might wind up being the only girl in her class with a cauliflower ear, caused by an affliction known as *telephonitis*. While science has little to say about it, I gather from talking to other parents that it is a disease common to teen-agers the country over. Patty has a violent case.

It puzzles me what Patty can talk about for an hour and a half to someone with whom she has been in class all day, not to mention forty-five minute rides on the same school bus. I beg of you, all you fathers and mothers who read this, tell me what can they talk about? They speak a subject and a language all their own and some-day, if I'm lucky, perhaps I'll understand. I know that I'd better because I have five more daughters to go!

But I also wonder . . . could Patty have inherited a form of *telephonitis* from me? Is it hereditary? After all, while I do not use a phone a great deal, I do blab away at a microphone four hours every day. And my wife says Patty's a spitting image of me, on the temperamental side, although I deny being temperamental. It's just the way I am. Me, the victim of *microphonitis;* Patty Ann, the victim of *telephonitis*.

Child Number Two is Mary Elizabeth, known as Beth. The second half of our Irish twins, the older a blonde, the younger a brunette and already, at thirteen, showing all the signs of growing up to be a real beauty. She has a great personality and about the only way in which she takes after me is in her fondness for food. This has brought us close together. Beth enjoys getting into the kitchen with me, and when we're doing a beef stew or whatever she'll peel the potatoes, scrape the carrots and even peel the onions, although I try to save her that tearful task. We've had a lot of fun putting dishes together. She has recently discovered the cake and cookie mixes, and she often has a fine time all by herself in the kitchen. She'll soon graduate to true cooking—preparation from scratch. She truly enjoys the results of cooking, which is what got first her grandfather and then me started on the kick. I have high hopes that when she's ready to take over her wifely duties she'll need no Mr. Parris to putter around the kitchen, as her mother did.

Beth has all the traits that a true lover of food must have, particularly a willingness to try anything once. She'll sample anything that I ever bring home—pig's feet; limburger; bierkäse; clams in all sizes, shapes, forms and possibilities: minced, steamed, in shell, out of shell, cooked or raw. Beth may not like them, not even to look at, but unlike all the other girls in the family, she'll at least give me a break and taste them. She's an adventuress at heart, and one of the prime requirements of a good cook is not being afraid to try things. Experiment. That's how you find out.

Catherine Jean is our third young lady. Cathy is twelve, the jolly one, the one with the greatest sense of humor. And she needs it, too, because being the third girl on the totem pole, she was the first one to be lorded over by older sisters. So Cathy is very much the up and down girl, flying on a cloud one minute, griping her head off the next. Basically, though, she's a very happy youngster. She gets along very well in school, but in a kitchen . . . oh my! Even including Linda, the baby in the family, Cathy is the clumsiest thing I've ever watched. She can make mistakes with a salt or pepper shaker. She can even get mixed up transferring sugar from a bowl to a dish of corn flakes.

Why, at the moment even Cathy's hair doesn't know where it's going. Right now it's sort of a washed-out blonde, and I believe it's slowly changing to a darker color. My guess is that Cathy will grow up to be a brownette one of these days, and a lovely one too.

Like her two older sisters, Cathy is an excellent dancer and has a great yen for theatricals. The girls often stage an after-dinner show for Mother and Dad, and their take-offs on some of the present-day TV commercials are pretty funny. They display thought and certainly a great sense of humor and an idea of the fine art of burlesque. I mean that in the old sense of the word, when burlesque was synonymous with satire. Burlesque, in the old days, took scenes out of the Broadway shows and turned them around to make them ridiculous and outlandishly funny. That was true burlesque, and that's what the girls do wonderfully at these after-dinner shows of theirs. The pratfalls are truly magnificent. The baggy pants and the big noses are out of this world. The pie-in-the-face routines are gorgeous, and they all go to prove that there's a great deal of showmanship wrapped up in Cathy.

Which reminds me of Ernie Kovacs and my favorite pie-in-the-face routine. I must digress to tell about that.

I numbered the late Ernie as one of my very good friends and he, I think, put the pie to the funniest use I've ever seen. He had that screwy television series before he went into the movies. It was at the time that the Coty Girl newspaper and magazine ads and TV commercials were the biggest thing on Madison Avenue. Readers will probably remember the old commercial that was all the rage. It opened by showing a floppy hat, very feminine but very large. The brim of the hat would tilt up and underneath was this gorgeous face which would coo, very softly, and sweetly, "Hi, I'm the Coty Girl." Then would come the commercial touting the products made by the Coty Company.

Well, I was watching one night, waiting for the Ernie Kovacs show to come on, when suddenly the screen went black and remained that way for much longer than usual. I thought, and I'm sure a few million other television viewers did too, that something had gone wrong with the set. I was just getting up to adjust it when it lit up again and on the screen came the big beautiful hat and the gorgeous thing lifted up her head. She started to speak. She got as far as "Hi, I'm the . . ."

And then—Pow! a pie right in the puss!

Well, I fell right out of the chair and rolled on the floor howling until I thought my sides would split.

45

That's pie-in-the-face comedy. And that, I think, was the greatest use of the routine that I'd ever seen. That was Ernie Kovacs' type of humor, and I know that ever since his untimely death he's probably had the angels rolling in the aisles.

Speaking of Ernie, speaking of pie, you'll find a recipe for a chiffon pie on page 190 that would be perfect for throwing but far better for eating. What's nicest about it, other than the flavor, is that it requires no baking. It's a perfect pie to make with six little helpers because there is very little chance of anyone being burned.

Speaking of girls brings us to Child Number Four.

Her name is Susan and she is a nine-year-old blonde version of her mother. When no one else knows where to find a veil in order to get to Mass on time on Sunday, Susan knows. When no one else can find shoes or a dress or socks or undies, little Susan has laid out everything for herself the night before. Her hair is immaculate. Everything is neat, tidy and in exactly the right place.

Sue is a vain little creature. She spends hours in front of her little-girl mirror in her room. She's meticulous, a carbon copy of her mother, and with a wordy command of the English language, too. I think Sue could wind up as a writer or perhaps as a teacher. She's something of a loner, which I'm told is also a writer's trait. While her sisters and their friends often congregate in groups, Susan can frequently be found in her room, drawing or writing or prettying up, and perfectly content all by herself. Sometimes we think she's trying to tell us that she somewhat disapproves of the raging mob that we have around here. But Sue is by no means a recluse—she likes her fun, too.

That brings us to our fifth wheel, Nancy, a brunette who reminds me very much of my sister Betty. Nancy is eight now and has the greatest smile and a very dry sense of humor. She's quite a teaser.

Nancy likes to help, especially on a Saturday or a Sunday morning. Years of getting up at about three in the morning to get me into the studio at six has made an early riser of me, even on my days off. So, I'll be down in the kitchen, starting breakfast for the tribe, when there'll be a patter of feet and Nancy will peek in, asking what she can do to help. Not even Beth, who loves the kitchen, does that. Not that early in the morning.

Then Nancy does anything that I ask her to do. Bring me a dish, butter or bacon or eggs from the refrigerator. And at night, when I go to bed . . . (it's awful, a grown man going to bed before his six little daughters, but that's the kind of life I'm forced to lead) . . . anyhow at night, after I'm in bed, it's Nancy or Sue who bring me a dish of ice cream or a piece of fruit. They say it so sweetly: "Help put you to sleep, Daddy."

Nancy's a delightful little girl. And, though it's difficult to tell at so early an age, I think she'll have theatrical aspirations too. Nancy gets along well with her sisters. While she by no means takes a back seat, she would rather back down than fight too hard. But only to a point. And when that point is reached she can put up a pretty good battle.

And now we come to Number Six, the last in the litter, the blockbuster, the tiger, Linda Marie! I think that if Allie Sherman, coach of the New York Football Giants, could see her, he'd say: "Gee, my worries are over if she'll just stay the way she is, but grow up to be a boy!" She's a real husky, and the main thing that I can say about her so far as food is concerned is that she can partake of it in copious quantities.

One hot summer day all the girls and what seemed at the time to be one hundred or two hundred of their friends were making the most of our backyard pool and I, as always, had been pressed into service to keep them supplied with grilled hamburgers and hot dogs and all the other things that it takes to keep an army going. (You'll find lots of their favorite recipes in the outdoor section beginning on page 171.)

I was squatted down on my haunches doing something to the charcoal grill when Linda, wringing wet, came over and patted me on the cheek and said, "You sure are a good cooker, Daddy." It was the nicest compliment I've ever received from her. But to this day I still don't know if it came from her heart or from her stomach.

That's our Linda. She's six now, with dark hair and the face of a saint but the personality of a little devil. And she's the nemesis of her older sisters. Being low girl on the totem pole she has developed into pretty much of a tomboy. In self-defense, I guess. I'm sure she'll outgrow it because no one with so sweet a face and so many feminine qualities could long remain a tomboy.

She's quite a personality girl, and quite a mama's girl, yet also fond of daddy. But when the chips are down it's mama that she'll run to. I think perhaps Barbara has fostered that, knowing Linda probably will be our last child. Like all mothers, she's trying to hold on to the baby as long as she can.

And there you have The Six Sterling Sisters. What an act they would be if vaudeville ever came back! And what eaters they are! One thing they'll never be is one of the Cratchit children when we cast Dickens' Christmas Carol every holiday season at Saint Aloysius School. We know, we've tried. They're sparkling, they're scintillating, they're sensational, but skinny none of them will ever be! Yes, as parental casting directors in any number of school plays, we've learned just how healthy they are.

Thank God they're all healthy, they've had a minimum of illnesses (nothing ever serious), and they're the answer to all of this proud papa's problems. I know that when we are all seated around the dinner table and I'm feeling low because of an accumulation of things that happened that day or that week or that month all I have to do is look around me. I see those six faces of those six very normal, very alive youngsters and I always realize how much I have to be thankful for and I snap right out of it.

It's quite a sight when the six of them take over the kitchen to whip up a batch of cookies. Out comes this, out comes that, in goes this, in goes that. "Do this!" says Beth. "Watch out!" warns Patty. "Ouch!" cries Cathy. But out of the turmoil and confusion come quite delightful cookies. I particularly recommend their Gingerbread and Raisin Honey Cookies. (Recipes on pages 188 and 189.)

Cookie making and putting the finishing touches to packaged cake mixes (which, by the way, are getting more like grandma used to make) are excellent means of introducing girls—and I guess boys, too—to a stove and to the kitchen in general. There is only a minimum amount of things that can go wrong, the trouble they can get into can easily be cleaned up and, when it comes to the stove, either Barbara or I manage to find an excuse for peeking into the kitchen along about the time it needs lighting. And one of us usually is just on the other side of a wall while the stove is in use, ready to jump through the door if necessary. But it never has been necessary. The girls do well. The cookies taste good, and they find that eating them is worth the bother of preparation. That's the way all cooking should be. Once children learn that, they're on the way to becoming *real* cooks.

Aside from a good wife and lovely children, there were always four things that I wanted most out of life. First, never having had one, I wanted a home of my own; second a room with a pool table; third a wine cellar; and last but far, far from least, a kitchen of my own. Our present house gives me all of these, and I count myself very lucky indeed to have them. Very lucky but, even more, very thankful.

The pool room, the wine cellar and the kitchen are all close by each other, along with an oversize rumpus room, in the basement. This is great for entertaining, particularly the informal kind that is about all we're able to do because of my hours. Formal, upstairs, best linen, company-is-coming dinners don't happen often in the Sterling household.

On a Saturday afternoon in the winter I'll have a couple of friends in for a game of pool, a few drinks and a late lunch that I don't have to walk more than twenty feet to prepare. On occasions such as that, our favorite food is Mexican, particularly chili. I have collected several good Mexican recipes and you'll find them all in the recipe section.

Several new-found friends during the past couple of years have tried the Sterling-style cuisine, and I think the fact that they still permit me to work with them at WHN constitutes some semblance of proof that the recipes I've amassed over the years were worth the effort.

It was in January 1967 that I moved over to the peace and tranquility of WHN after eighteen years at CBS, and it was one of the happiest things that has happened to me in many a moon. Working there seems more like my early days in radio, which were so enjoyable. WHN is one of the Storer group of radio and television stations scattered around the United States but, because it is not nearly so large as the vast CBS network, I get to see—and better still I get to know—everyone I work for and with. The Storer management and John Moler, president and general manager of WHN, have put together a great staff. I'm complimented to be part of it.

Yes, they're my new-found friends at WHN and, I'm extremely happy to say, not only do they like the food I cook but some of them even prevailed upon their wives to contribute some excellent recipes for me to try in my kitchen at home. Some are in this book.

There's one gent at WHN who is a very old friend . . . so much so that he feels he can take liberties not only with me but also with this literary masterpiece. I'm talking about the man who goes on the air when I go off, none other than Jim "Old Golden Throat" Ameche. Jim and I kid each other quite a bit on our respective shows, but that guy even tried to carry his practical joking into the pages of as sterling an effort as *The Sterling Cookbook!* It happened like this:

I dropped by Jim's East Side apartment with a photographer to take pictures of Old Golden Throat and his lovely wife, Mary. We went into the kitchen and gathered around the stove. The photog posed us just so, then told us to smile and watch the birdie. And that's when my friend, my colleague, my rival for commercial sponsors, pulled a jar of spaghetti sauce—made by one of his sponsors, of course!—out from under his jacket and held it up large as life to dominate the picture!

But I don't have a big nose for nothing. Suddenly I had to sneeze, and I pulled out my king-size handkerchief, which somehow ended up covering the jar. If Jim Ameche ends up losing a sponsor . . . well, all I can say is that there's room for a spaghetti sauce on *my* show.

I must warn you, though, that it would be hard for a sauce to be as good as that made by Carmen Prelee, whose husband, WHN news director Michael Prelee, is living evidence of the fact that she's a wondrous cook. You'll find Carmen's recipes both for the sauce and for meat balls in the recipe section. And take a good look at the recipes. You'll discover that Carmen does not make either of them on top of the stove. She bakes them in the oven instead! That simple little switch does wonders for their flavor, but that is not Carmen's only reason for cooking them that way. There are these added benefits, she says: the meatballs stay round, the sauce never scorches, kids can't pull the pot over on themselves, and she can leave the oven on even when she goes out so that dinner cooks while she is busily doing other things.

Another gal with a marked flair for cookery is Jane DeFreitas, if the bounciness of newscaster-husband Dick DeFreitas is any criterion.

Just as Carmen (who vows that someday she will write a cookbook) is known far and wide for her culinary skill, so too is Jane famed for her kitchen creativity. She always has a homemade pound cake in the freezer, ready for quick doctoring either into a mocha iced cake (Dick's favorite) or a strawberry shortcake (see Cakes and Pastries section) if unexpected company comes.

And her green salads are out of this world—thanks, so help me, to a washing machine! What Jane does is this:

In the morning she shops for Boston lettuce, iceberg lettuce, celery (for this salad she uses only the tops), escarole, chicory, French endive and watercress. In the afternoon she washes and pat-dries them, puts them into a mesh bag and spins them in the washer, then removes them and stores them in a plastic bag for last-minute tossing. When it is nearly time to serve, she adds the dressing (her Roquefort dressing recipe is on page 78) and, to prevent wilting, only at the last minute sprinkles the greens with salt. Jane, by the way, omits the watercress when she plans to use the Roquefort dressing. She says their flavors clash.

I guess most of you have heard of, and perhaps been part of, progressive dinners. But if you have not, I'd suggest that you try one sometime, particularly if you like to entertain and if you like a bit of adventure in your eating.

We have a nice circle of friends up there on our hill and in the valleys in and around New Canaan. No great-name people, no headliners, nobody whose names you would recognize. But good friends, good neighbors. The kind of people anyone would like to be among. And we have our progressive dinners quite often. We have fun. Lots of fun. But very little work.

The first course is served in John and Jane's house, the second in Dick and Debbie's house, the third in Matthew and Mable's, and so forth. How many courses depends on how many couples are involved. It might be four, eight, ten or twelve. But four is what we think is best.

In House Number One we have cocktails and canapes. Then we drive on to House Number Two for the soup or appetizer. At House Number Three comes the main course, at House Number Four the dessert-and-coffee course, after-dinner drinks, dancing, cards, or just sitting around talking and listening to good music.

We try to remember two things: To keep rotating so that each host and hostess has his or her turn at each course. And second, and very, very important (particularly if you're having wine or some such exuberance-stimulating drink with each course), is to include either the Mayor or Chief of Police and his wife on your progressive dinner list! It's amazing how they can keep things from ending up the way no festive evening ever should. With them around, no one ever drinks too much, no one ever plows a car into a ditch, no one sings songs on a strange doorstep at three o'clock in the morning.

Try it. It is great fun.

Speaking of trying things . . .

I hope that you will try all the recipes in this book, because after all, that is why this book was written. But in trying them, remember that no recipe ever created was meant to be followed verbatim, grain for grain, pinch for pinch, dash for dash. If all of our tastes were that much the same then there would be no need for this cookbook or any other cookbook. All some food processor would have to do would be to compress the ingredients into cubes, mark one breakfast, another lunch, a third one dinner and there we'd all be. Eating alike, drinking alike, thinking alike, acting alike, suffering alike.

One of my most pleasant tasks in recent years has been covering the openings of the Royal Box at the Americana Hotel in New York because it involves superb food as well as meeting a host of stars who appear there. The list sounds almost like a *Who's Who of Show Business*—Harry Belafonte, Caterina Valente, The 5th Dimension, Ella Fitzgerald, Peggy Lee, Eddie Fisher, and many others. Perhaps the most memorable night was the one when Billy Eckstine was unable to make his opening and had volunteer substitutes. We saw and heard in that single evening Sammy Davis, Jr., Bill Cosby, Tony Bennett, Robert Goulet, and Jack E. Leonard.

For these gala events Barbara comes into town and joins me. Because of my broadcast schedule, we stay in town and on those mornings I can rot my life away in bed until all of five o'clock!

The food is particularly good at the Americana, as I have often told our host for these enjoyable evenings, Preston Robert Tisch, president of Loew's Hotels, whose success with the Americana I attribute, in part, to his excellent taste. Even though the kitchen serves thousands of people daily, a consistently high standard is maintained, indicating constant supervision and good management. Some time ago Bob introduced me to his head chef, Marcel Haentzler, whose office, with its liberal coverage of framed culinary awards and diplomas, bears witness to his claim to an international reputation among gourmets. You will note one of his most recent awards, a most impressive medallion, worn around his neck in the photograph with Bob Tisch and me. He was generous enough to give me some of his favorite recipes and also gave permission to share them with you.

Whenever you have an extra-special occasion and want to serve superb dishes, follow Chef Haentzler's recipes to the letter. They are on pages 95 and 162. Then turn down the lights, put on some soft music, light the candles, and serve the dinner. If you like, you can have fun pretending that you are attending an opening night at the glamorous Royal Box.

So have at it. Have fun. My recipes reflect my taste, and I suggest that you use them mainly as a guide—add something, subtract something, change this, alter that. Do to a recipe whatever you know your family will like best. That's what makes for good eating.

And now, as we come to the close of the narrative section of *The Sterling Cookbook*, I think it's particularly appropriate that I sign off just as I've done on radio every day for twenty years . . . and in the same words: Have a good day, remember you can make it a better day for somebody else.

RECIPES

The recipes in this all-important part of the book profess to do only one thing: acquaint you with the dishes that I like to cook and that my wife, daughters, friends and I like to eat. I don't know what the doctors have to say about my friends, but I do know that my wife and daughters are healthy and so I guess my cooking agrees with them. Therefore I do not hesitate to recommend these recipes to you.

I could not begin to thank by name all of the people—hotel and club managers, professional chefs, restaurant proprietors, teacher-cooks, et al.—who over the years have given me pointers and recipes. And so I've done the next best thing: to the best of my ability and memory, in each recipe I've identified the source, usually in the title.

APPETIZERS, HORS D'OEUVRES, and CANAPÉS

German Tomato Herring Spread

1 14- or 15-oz. oval can tomato herring or tomato sardines
1 medium onion, diced
1 cup potato chips, crumbled

Paprika for garnish
1 cucumber, unpeeled and sliced

Empty contents of can, liquid included, into mixing bowl. Mash fish coarsely with a fork. Stir in onion. Refrigerate until ready to serve. At that time, gently stir in the potato chips. Garnish with paprika if desired and serve with cucumber slices, using them as you would crackers. Serves 6.

Eggs Stuffed with Lobster

1 lb. cooked lobster meat
½ tb. capers
1 tb. grated onion
1 tb. chopped stuffed olives
⅔ cup mayonnaise
½ tsp. monosodium glutamate

Juice of 1 small lemon
1 tb. chili sauce
18 hard-boiled eggs
Parsley for garnish

Combine lobster meat and capers and chop fine. Transfer to mixing bowl and stir in grated onion and chopped olives. Add mayonnaise, monosodium glutamate, lemon juice and chili sauce.

Stir until thoroughly blended. Slice eggs in half lengthwise, remove yolks and fill the white cavities with the lobster mixture. Garnish with parsley. (Yolks may be used in Yolk-Stuffed Mushroom Caps recipe that follows.) Yield: 36.

Yolk-Stuffed Mushroom Caps

About 1 lb. fresh raw mushrooms, no more than 1
inch in diameter
½ lb. cream cheese

1 tb. Worcestershire sauce
18 yolks of hard-boiled
eggs

Remove mushroom stems. Rub each cap gently but thoroughly with damp cloth until completely clean, or peel carefully with paring knife. Set aside. Blend cream cheese and Worcestershire sauce to a smooth consistency. Mash egg yolks with a fork, combine with cheese mixture and stir until thoroughly blended. Stuff each mushroom cap with mixture, chill and serve. Yield: very roughly, from 30 to 50.

Shrimp Toast

½ lb. raw shrimp
4 water chestnuts, finely
minced
1 tsp. salt
½ tsp. sugar

1 tb. cornstarch
1 egg, slightly beaten
6 slices white bread, 2 or
3 days old
2 cups peanut oil

Shell and devein shrimp; wash, drain and mince finely. Mix shrimp thoroughly in a bowl with minced water chestnuts, salt, sugar and cornstarch. Stir in egg until combination is well mixed. Trim crusts from bread slices and cut each slice into 4 triangles. Spread 1 tsp. of shrimp mixture over 1 side of each triangle. Heat oil in 8″ or 10″

deep frying pan to 375°F. With fork, gently lower triangles into oil, shrimp side down and taking care not to crowd. Cook for 1 minute, then turn triangles with a spatula and fry for a few seconds more, until crisp and golden brown. Drain on absorbent paper towels and serve immediately. Makes 24 toast bits.

NOTE: Shrimp toast can be made ahead, stored in refrigerator and reheated in oven at time of serving. Or they can be frozen and reheated without thawing.

Grapefruit and Crab Cocktail

1 6½-oz. (about) can, or 1 cup cooked crab meat, chilled and drained	Lettuce
	1 cup mayonnaise
2 cups, or 1 1-lb. can, grapefruit segments, chilled and drained	2 tbs. catsup
	1 tb. lemon juice
	Tabasco sauce to taste

Flake crab meat. Sprinkle with just enough lemon juice to moisten, and alternate with layers of grapefruit in cocktail cups or glasses lined with lettuce. Blend mayonnaise, catsup, remaining lemon juice and tabasco sauce into a smooth sauce and pour over. Serves 6 to 8 depending on size of cups or glasses.

Ham Fans

1 3-oz. can chopped mushrooms	6 Parker House rolls, or rolls of your choice
1 4½-oz. can deviled ham	

Place mushrooms and deviled ham in small bowl and mix until well blended. Slit rolls from top almost to bottom so that they open up like fans, with each slice about ½-inch thick. Spread ham-and-mushroom mixture on both sides of each slice, place rolls on greased cookie sheet and bake about 10 minutes in preheated 400°F. oven. Yield: 6.

Guacamole

A Mexican Avocado Dip

2 very ripe medium-size avocados

2 medium tomatoes, chopped

1 medium onion or 1 bunch green onions (scallions), chopped fine

Green peeled chilis, chopped, to taste

½ cup finely choped peanuts

Wine vinegar, to taste

Salt, to taste

Cut avocados in half, discard seeds, scoop the pulp into a bowl and mash with a fork until smooth. Add all other ingredients and mix well. Yield: about 2 to 3 cups of dip.

NOTE: Prepare Guacamole just before serving; otherwise it will turn black.

Almond Balls

1 cup slivered almonds

¼ lb. cream cheese or pimento cheese

1 tb. cream

Combine cheese and cream, shape into balls about ¾ inch in diameter, roll in almonds, chill and serve. Yield: about 16.

Bacon Balls

4 strips bacon, crumbled

¼ lb. cream cheese or pimento cheese

1 tb. cream

Fry bacon until crisp. Drain and crumble into small pieces. Combine cheese and cream, shape into balls about ¾ inch in diameter, roll in bacon, chill and serve. Yield: 16.

Liver Balls

1 5-oz. (about) can liver pâté	¼ lb. cream cheese
	1 tsp. minced onion

Combine all ingredients, shape into balls about ¾ inch in diameter, chill and serve. Yield: 16.

Chicken Balls

1 cup leftover chicken, broken into fine pieces	¼ lb. cream cheese
	1 tb. cream

Combine cheese and cream, shape into balls about ¾ inch in diameter, roll in chicken, chill and serve. Yield: about 32.

Anchovy Balls

¼ lb. anchovy paste	¼ cup minced parsley
1 hard-boiled egg, chopped	
½ tsp. Worcestershire sauce	

Combine all ingredients, mixing well. Shape into balls about ¾ inch in diameter, chill and serve. Yield: about 20.

Anchovy Spread

1 2-oz. can anchovy fillets, undrained	1 tb. finely chopped onion
½ lb. cream cheese	

Empty anchovy liquid into bowl. Place fillets on cutting board, chop as fine as possible, then mash. Add fillets to bowl containing liquid. Also add cheese and chopped onion and mix until blended into spreading consistency. Serve with toast or crackers. Yield: about 40.

Shrimp and Poultry Stuffing Tidbits

(This goes nicely with cocktails while a holiday bird is roasting)

2 6½-oz. cans tiny shrimp, drained	¼ can cheddar cheese soup
2 cups bread-base poultry stuffing	

Combine all ingredients, mix well and shape into firm balls ½ to 1 inch in diameter. Place shrimp balls on ovenware (lightly greased) that will fit into your oven while bird is roasting. Bake at poultry temperature until golden brown. If balls are firm enough, they can be strung on skewers and placed across end of roasting pan. Yield: about 36.

VARIATIONS:
1. After shrimp balls are formed and before baking they can be rolled in a little catsup, covered with cornflake crumbs and then baked as above.
2. Undiluted canned mushroom soup may be substituted for cheddar cheese soup.

Molded Cheese, Caviar and Wine

½ pint cottage cheese	½ tsp. powdered tarragon, or more to taste
½ pint sour cream	

1 clove garlic, crushed	1 tb. unflavored gelatin
1 tsp. Worcestershire sauce	3 tbs. sherry wine
Dash Tabasco sauce	1 4-oz. (about) jar caviar
Dash dark soy sauce	Juice of 1 small lemon

Combine cheese, cream, tarragon, garlic and Worcestershire sauce, tabasco and soy sauces in blender and mix until smooth. Combine gelatin and sherry wine, place over hot water and stir until gelatin dissolves. Add to blender mixture, and whip until light. Pour into lightly greased mold, chill 24 hours and turn onto serving dish. Combine caviar with lemon juice and spoon over mold. Serves 6 if you have it for a luncheon main dish or teatime snack. But it goes best on an appetizer table.

NOTE: It may take practice, but the best way to turn a cold mold onto a serving dish without breaking is to wrap damp, hot towels around the mold-form when it comes from the refrigerator, place serving dish on top of it and quickly turn both upside down.

Chicken Liver Pâté

2 tsps. butter	1 tb. grated onion
¼ lb. chicken livers	Salt and red pepper to taste
1 tb. brandy	

Melt butter in skillet. Add livers and sauté gently. Transfer to chopper and chop well. Then transfer to bowl and mash well. Add all other ingredients and mix into a spreadable paste. Chill and serve with toast bits or crackers. Yield: 18 to 24.

VARIATIONS: 3 ozs. cream cheese and 1 tsp. cream may be added to mashed livers along with all the other ingredients and mixed in with them.

Sherry wine may be substituted for brandy.

Deviled Shrimp

½ cup white wine
½ cup wine vinegar
1 tsp. horseradish
2 tbs. prepared mustard
2 tbs. catsup
1 tsp. paprika

¼ tsp. cayenne pepper
1 tsp. salt
1 clove garlic, crushed
1 cup salad oil
1 lb. cleaned, cooked shrimp

Combine all ingredients except shrimp in glass mixing bowl and beat until well blended. Add shrimp, stir gently to assure complete saturation, and marinate in refrigerator for 3 or 4 hours. Drain shrimp, arrange in lettuce-lined bowl and place on appetizer table.

N O T E : If you use jumbo shrimp you'll have about 16 to the pound; small, you'll have about 60. The jumbo cost more, but there's far more work to cleaning the little ones. You might say, then, that medium-size shrimp strike a happy medium between cost and work.

Shrimp Dill Dip

¾ cup salt
1 tb. pickling spice
¼ tsp. red pepper
1 tb. celery seed
6 sprigs fresh dill
½-inch piece Chinese ginger root

1 large onion, sliced
1 stalk celery, quartered
2 cloves garlic
3 qts. water
2 lbs. fresh raw shrimp, unshelled

Place all ingredients except shrimp in large pot. Boil vigorously for 5 minutes, add shrimp and continue to boil for another 10 minutes. Remove shrimp, set aside to cool. Then remove shrimp shells, leaving tails intact. Refrigerate while preparing dill sauce (recipe follows).

Dill Sauce

3 tbs. lemon juice
¾ cup olive oil
½ clove garlic, crushed

1 tb. chopped fresh dill
½ tsp. dry mustard
Salt to taste

Combine all ingredients in bowl and stir until smoothly blended. Pour into dip dish and set in center of serving platter. Surround with shrimp (above) and serve.

Shrimp and Anchovy Dip

1 lemon, sliced
3 peppercorns
1 cup white wine

1 cup water
Salt to taste
1 lb. raw shrimp, unshelled

Combine all ingredients, except shrimp, in a pot and bring to a boil. Add unshelled shrimp and simmer until pink. Allow to cool in liquid; then shell, taking care not to remove tails. Place in refrigerator while preparing anchovy sauce dip (recipe follows).

Anchovy Sauce

6 anchovy fillets
2 tbs. vinegar
2 tbs. olive oil
1 clove garlic, minced
1 tb. chopped celery

1 tb. chopped chives
1 tb. chopped dill
1 tb. salt
1 tb. Dijon mustard

Mash anchovies in a mixing bowl, add all other ingredients and mix until thoroughly blended. Transfer to dip dish, surround with shrimp and serve.

Spiked Melon Balls

2 melons*
¼ tsp. ginger
½ tsp. citric acid (sour salt)
¼ tsp. monosodium glutamate

Rind of 1 small lemon, grated
½ tsp. freshly ground black pepper
¼ tsp. salt
Mint sprigs for garnish

Cut melon meat into balls with a ball cutter and place in mixing bowl. In separate bowl combine all other ingredients, except mint, and mix until it is oily-looking but coarse-textured. Sprinkle mixture over melon balls and toss gently until all are coated. Place on serving dish, garnish with mint sprigs, spear balls with cocktail picks and serve.

Cherry-Sherry Clams

1 pt. cherry tomatoes
1 tb. butter or margarine
1 small onion, minced
1 small green pepper, minced
1 tb. dry sherry

1 7-oz. (about) can minced clams, drained
¼ lb. mild cheddar cheese, grated
¼ cup catsup
¼ tsp. Tabasco sauce

Cut tops off cherry tomatoes in about ⅛-inch slices and save. Carefully scoop out the tomato pulp, being sure not to pierce skin. Set tomatoes aside. Melt butter or margarine in heavy skillet, add onion and pepper and sauté until onion is lightly browned. Combine all remaining ingredients, add to sautéed vegetables and cook over medium heat until cheese melts. Fill cherry tomatoes with mixture, put tops back in place, arrange on platter and place on hors d'oeuvres table. Makes about 24.

* Any melons in season will do; but for appearance only, 2 of contrasting colors are best.

Chinese Cocktail Mushrooms

3 lbs. mushrooms	4 garlic cloves, chopped
1 cup sherry wine	4 tsps. salt
12 juniper berries, crushed	2/3 cup sugar
1 large onion, chopped	1 1/3 cup soy sauce

Wipe mushrooms clean with a damp cloth, remove stems and place caps in earthenware or glass bowl. Combine all other ingredients in a pot, bring to a boil and immediately pour over mushroom caps. Cover and let stand in a cool place for from 24 to no more than 36 hours. Remove caps from marinade, rinse in cold water, spear with cocktail picks and serve.

Bacon 'n' Cheese Pie

12 strips bacon	Pinch of nutmeg
4 eggs	1 cup grated cheddar
2 cups heavy cream	cheese, mild or sharp to
Salt and pepper to taste	taste
1/4 tsp. sugar	1 unbaked 9-inch pie shell,
Pinch of cayenne pepper	chilled

Place bacon in skillet. While it is frying, combine eggs, cream, salt, pepper, sugar, cayenne pepper and nutmeg in a bowl and beat with rotary beater until thoroughly blended. When bacon is crisp, place on absorbent paper to drain, then crumble and spread in pie shell to cover bottom. Top the bacon with grated cheese and then add all the egg-and-cream mixture to cover. Bake in 400°F. oven about 30 minutes or until knife tip inserted in pie filling comes out clean. Cut into appetizer-size wedges and serve while hot. Makes about 12 to 14 wedges.

Skewered Orange Shrimp, Oriental

1 tsp. sugar	¼ tsp. powdered ginger
1 cup bouillon, preferably vegetable	¼ tsp. salt
1 tb. sherry	8 jumbo shrimp, shelled
1 tb. soy sauce	8 tangerine sections
	8 small sweet pickles

Combine sugar, bouillon, sherry, soy sauce, ginger and salt, stir well and bring to a boil over low heat. Place shrimp, tangerine sections and pickles in glass bowl, top with the hot marinade, let stand to room temperature and then refrigerate 1 hour. Stir occasionally to assure uniform saturation. Alternate shrimp, tangerine and pickle on short skewers (about 4 inches long), preheat oven (or use charcoal grill) and broil about 4 inches from source of heat for approximately 8 minutes, turning as needed to assure uniform doneness. Use the marinade, either cold or reheated, as a dip. Serves 8.

N O T E : If you can find mandarin oranges, perhaps in an Oriental gourmet shop or Chinatown grocery, use them in place of tangerines.

Ned Pechairno's Marinated Mushrooms

1 lb. small button mushrooms	4 tbs. lemon juice
4 tbs. olive oil	2 tbs. brandy
¼ cup minced onion	2 tbs. minced parsley, preferably Italian
1 tsp. salt	
¼ tsp. black pepper, preferably freshly ground	

Wash mushrooms and parboil for 2 minutes. Drain and set aside. Heat oil in a skillet and sauté onions 3 minutes; add mushrooms and sauté 2 minutes more. Stir in salt, pepper and lemon juice. Cover and cook over low heat 5 minutes. Stir in brandy. Chill in refrigerator for 3 hours. Sprinkle with parsley and serve either alone as an appetizer or a vegetable side dish, or best, as part of an antipasto. Serves 4 to 6.

Ned Pechairno's Peppers with Anchovy Sauce

6 green peppers	1 garlic clove
1 tb. butter	8 anchovy fillets, minced
3 tbs. olive oil	

Wash peppers, cover with water in a saucepan, bring to a boil, remove from heat and let stand 10 minutes. Drain and peel off the skin, cut into thin slices, discard seeds and white fibers and set aside. Heat butter and oil in a skillet, add garlic and minced anchovy and cook 2 minutes over low heat, stirring constantly. Discard garlic and pour contents of skillet over pepper slices. Chill in refrigerator for 3 hours. Serve either alone or as part of an antipasto. Serves 4 to 6.

Ned Pechairno's Shrimp and Mushroom Mix

1 lb. firm white mushrooms	¼ tsp. salt
½ cup olive oil	1 lb. small shrimp, cooked
4 tbs. lemon juice	and cleaned
½ tsp. black pepper, preferably fresh ground	2 tbs. minced parsley, preferably Italian
⅛ tsp. minced garlic	

Wash mushrooms and remove stems. Parboil 2 minutes, drain on absorbent paper and then slice mushrooms paper thin into a glass bowl. Add oil, lemon juice, pepper and garlic, stir once or twice and set in refrigerator to marinate for at least 2 hours. Stir several times while marinating. Remove from refrigerator, add salt and shrimp, stir and let stand at room temperature for 30 minutes. Garnish with parsley. Serves 4 to 6.

Ned Pechairno's Anchovies on Toast

3 cans anchovy fillets
2 tbs. minced onion
2 garlic cloves, minced
3 tbs. minced parsley, preferably Italian

2 tbs. olive oil
1 tb. lemon juice
18 rounds or triangles of buttered toast

Place contents of 3 cans of anchovy fillets, oil included, into mixing bowl and mash into a paste with a fork. Mix in the remaining ingredients, spread on the toast rounds or triangles, place on buttered baking pan and bake 5 minutes at 475° F. Serve at once. Yield: 18.

SOUPS, SALADS,
and VEGETABLES

Chilled Cream of Crab Soup

½ lb. crabmeat   1 tsp. paprika
4 cups chicken broth   Dash of pepper
2 tsps. lemon juice   1 tsp. salt
2 tsps. chopped onion   1 pint cream

Place crabmeat, 2 cups chicken broth, lemon juice, onion, paprika, pepper and salt in blender for 1 minute. Pour remaining 2 cups broth in pot, add blender mix and simmer for 10 minutes. Cool to room temperature. Thoroughly mix in the cream and chill in refrigerator about 1 hour before serving. Serves 4.

N O T E : Diced cucumber and chopped parsley make nice garnishes.

Creamed Corn Soup

3 tbs. butter   ¾ tsp. salt
1 thinly sliced onion   ⅛ tsp. pepper
3 cups corn kernels, pref-   ¼ tsp. celery salt
   erably fresh, but drained   ¼ tsp. parsley flakes
   if from a can   1 cup sour cream
6 cups milk   Paprika for garnish

Melt butter at low heat in heavy skillet. Add onion and corn and cook slowly for 10 minutes, stirring fairly often. Transfer to blender, add 2 cups milk and whirl 1 minute. Transfer to top of double boiler, add remaining milk, salt, pepper, celery salt and parsley flakes and cook one-half hour. Remove from heat, stir in sour cream and serve at once. Garnish with paprika. Serves 6.

71

Fish Chowder

5 tbs. cooking oil, preferably olive oil
1 cup sliced leek
1 cup sliced celery
⅓ cup chopped parsley
1 large carrot, sliced
4 large potatoes, sliced

1 quart water
Salt to taste
2 lbs. assorted fish, bones
removed*
2 cups milk
2 cups light cream
Pepper to taste

In a heavy soup pot heat oil until it sizzles but does not smoke. Add leek, celery, parsley and carrot and sauté for 3 minutes, stirring occasionally. Add potatoes, water and salt and cook at low heat until potatoes are nearly tender, about 10–15 minutes. Add fish, cover pot and simmer 5 minutes. Then add milk, cream and pepper and heat to serving temperature. Serves 4.

N O T E : To thicken chowder, mix 1 tb. flour with 1 tb. oil and stir into chowder after it is removed from heat. When blended, reheat to boiling and serve.

Onion Soup

(Soupe à l'oignon gratinée)

(All good cooks appreciate a good onion soup, and Chef Haentzler gives the method to make it properly.)

12 onions (medium size)
4 tbs. butter
1 heaping tbs. flour
2 quarts stock (or salted
water)

6 to 8 slices French bread
⅔ cup grated gruyère
cheese

Slice onions fine and fry in butter, stirring frequently. As soon as they acquire a light color, sprinkle with flour and stir with a wooden spoon for 3 minutes. Place onions in a large pan (2½ quarts) and add

* Any fish, finned or shell, in season will do. An ideal combination is flounder, fresh tuna, crab meat and shrimp.

stock or water. Simmer gently for 20 minutes. Dry bread slices in oven and place in soup tureen or in individual bowls. Sprinkle each slice with grated cheese. Pour the soup over the bread.

Sprinkle the floating bread liberally with grated cheese once more, plus a little melted butter. Put under the broiler or in the oven and serve when cheese becomes golden. Serves 6 to 8.

Jim Mertikas' Special Salad

2 large purple onions, sliced thin	2 tbs. lemon juice
2 firm ripe tomatoes, sliced medium thin	¼ lb. feta cheese, crumbled
½ cup olive oil	2 tsps. oregano

Divide onion and tomato slices equally, or according to individual appetites, on 4 separate salad plates. Combine olive oil and lemon juice and spoon over each. Sprinkle with crumbled feta cheese and then with oregano. Let each guest cut salad bite-size, season with salt and pepper, and mix. Serves 4.

VARIATION: Bermuda onions and cold ricotta cheese may be substituted for the purple onions and feta cheese.

Cheese-Stuffed Tomato Salad

¼ cup French dressing, the lighter the better*	1 scallion or 1 very small onion, finely chopped
½ lb. sharp cheddar cheese, diced	6 firm ripe tomatoes
3 hard-cooked eggs, finely chopped	6 crisply firm lettuce leaves
¼ cup sweet pickle relish	1 tb. mayonnaise
¼ cup pimento, finely chopped	Chopped parsley for garnish

* Make sure the French dressing is a light variety and not the thick, syrupy type. See recipe on page 78.

Pour French dressing into glass mixing bowl. Add diced cheese, chopped eggs, pickle relish, chopped pimento and onion. Stir and let stand at room temperature for an hour. Carefully scoop out the tomato seeds and pulp, fill the hollows with the stuffing mixture and chill in refrigerator for about an hour. To serve, place each stuffed tomato on a lettuce leaf, top with a dab of mayonnaise and sprinkle with chopped parsley. Serves 6.

Caesar Salad

1 clove garlic, mashed
½ cup olive oil
1 beaten egg yolk
½ head lettuce, preferably romaine
½ bunch curly endive
1 cup garlic croutons (recipe follows)
1 2-oz. can anchovy fillets

1 beaten egg
¼ cup lemon juice
1 tsp. Worcestershire sauce
½ tsp. freshly ground black pepper
½ tsp. salt
½ cup grated Parmesan cheese, preferably freshly grated

Add garlic to olive oil and let stand. Pour beaten egg yolk into wooden bowl in which salad will be served. Break lettuce on top of that. Tear and add endive. Then add garlic croutons and anchovies. Strain oil to remove garlic, pour over the salad and, using wooden fork and spoon, toss lightly to coat the leaves both with oil and egg yolk. Combine all remaining ingredients except cheese, pour over the salad and toss once again, gently but thoroughly. Lastly sprinkle cheese over all. Serves 6.

VARIATION: Fry 6 slices of bacon until crisp. Drain, crumble and sprinkle over salad just before the cheese. Bacon may be used in place of or along with the anchovies.

Garlic Croutons

1 small loaf day-old French ¼ lb. butter
bread 1 tsp. garlic powder

Cut bread into ¼-inch slices. Dice each slice into ¼-inch cubes. Melt butter in saucepan and stir in the garlic powder. Pour into shallow baking pan and add bread cubes. Preheat oven to 350°F., slide in the baking pan and leave until brown, about 20 minutes, stirring often.

N O T E : Reserve croutons that you will not use in Caesar Salad for use another day in other dishes. They can be frozen.

Chef's Salad Bowl

1 clove garlic
10–12 lettuce leaves, preferably romaine
2 cups cooked ham, cut in
strips the size of wooden
matches
½ lb. American cheese, cut
as the ham is cut
1½ lbs. fresh asparagus,
cooked, drained and
chilled (canned could do)

2 cups peas, cooked and
chilled
1 bunch radishes, sliced
2 hard-boiled eggs, sliced
Salt and freshly ground
pepper to taste

Rub wooden salad bowl with garlic clove. Discard garlic and line bowl with lettuce leaves. In a separate bowl combine ham, cheese, asparagus, peas, radishes and eggs and then transfer to salad bowl. Allow each guest to add salt, pepper and French dressing (see recipe on page 78) to individual tastes. Serves 6.

N O T E : Cold julienned turkey and/or chicken may be added to salad or may be substituted for the ham. Swiss cheese may be substituted for the American cheese.

Mother MacGregor's Fresh-Caught Seafood Salad

1 lb. any fresh-caught fish, preferably white meat
6 black olives, chopped fine
3 celery stalks, chopped fine
½ cup mayonnaise
1 tb. lemon juice

6 large Jersey (or beef-steak) tomatoes
6 large crisp lettuce leaves
1 medium-sized cucumber, sliced but unskinned
12 scallions
12 radishes

Place a rack in a pot. Pour in about ½ inch water; place fish on rack, making sure it does not touch water. Cover and steam until flesh flakes easily when tested with a fork, about 4 to 7 minutes. Remove skin and bones, flake flesh and place in mixing bowl. Add olives, celery, mayonnaise, and lemon juice and mix with fork until well blended. Cut tops from tomatoes, scoop out pulp and save for other use. Fill each tomato with the fish mixture, and place on lettuce leaves on salad plates; arrange cucumber slices, scallions and radishes around each. Serves 6.

Frank Chacksfield's Avocado and Shrimp Salad

3 large avocados
Sprinkling of lemon juice
3 3-oz. (about) jars of baby shrimp

1 tb. French dressing
Fresh dill for garnish, if available

Cut avocados in half lengthwise. Discard stones and sprinkle lightly with lemon juice to keep pulp from turning black. Arrange ½ jar of shrimp in rows on each avocado half. Sprinkle each with no more than ½ tsp. French dressing, garnish with dill and serve. Serves 6.

Lima Bean Salad

1 lb. fresh lima beans
1 large onion, chopped
Salt and pepper to taste

⅓ cup olive oil
Juice of 1 lemon
½ tsp. oregano

Wash, shell and cook lima beans in boiling water until tender. Drain and place in mixing bowl along with all other ingredients except oregano. Toss lightly 5 or 6 times. Sprinkle with oregano and serve at once. Serves 4.

N O T E : Frozen beans may be used. If so, follow directions on package and then proceed with recipe.

Vegetable Salad, à la Jim Mertikas

½ head cabbage, shredded	Salt and pepper to taste
½ lb. string beans, cooked	4 tbs. vinegar
1 tb. capers	1 tsp. dry mustard
12 black Greek olives	6 tbs. olive oil
4 large beets, cooked and sliced (canned will do)	Oregano for garnish

Mix cabbage, beans, capers, olives and beets in a bowl and add salt and pepper to taste. Combine vinegar, mustard and olive oil and pour over vegetable mixture. Toss gently 3 or 4 times, garnish with oregano and serve. Serves 6.

Mixed Greek Salata with Sardines or Anchovies

½ head lettuce	8 black Greek olives
3 stalks celery, chopped (leaves included)	1 can imported sardines or anchovies
1 medium cucumber, quartered and sliced	Salt and pepper to taste
	⅓ cup olive oil
1 small onion, sliced thin	Juice of 2 lemons
2 medium tomatoes, halved and thinly sliced	¼ lb. feta cheese, crumbled*
½ green pepper, chopped	1 tsp. oregano

* If feta, a Greek-style goat's milk cheese, is not available, a dry, large-curd cottage or farmers' cheese makes a not-very-adequate but passable substitute.

Wash and thoroughly clean all vegetables. Drain. Break lettuce into 1-inch pieces and place in mixing bowl. Add all other vegetables and olives. Mix fairly well. Add sardines or anchovies (or both if you like) and mix some more. Add salt and pepper if desired and mix again. Combine olive oil and lemon juice, pour over contents of bowl and mix thoroughly until the ingredients are nicely coated. Sprinkle first with crumbled feta and then with oregano and serve. Serves 4.

French Dressing

2 tbs. sugar
1 tsp. salt
1 tsp. dry mustard
1 tsp. paprika
⅓ cup herb or wine vinegar

4 tbs. lemon juice
1 tb. finely grated onion
⅔ cup salad oil, preferably olive

Combine all ingredients in a 2-cup measuring pitcher. Stir once or twice and then pour into bottle or jar with screw-on cap and shake vigorously and well for about 1 minute. Makes about 1½ cups. Unused dressing may be refrigerated in bottle or jar with tight-fitting cover.

Jane DeFreitas' Roquefort Dressing

1 cup sour cream
¼ lb. Roquefort or blue cheese, crumbled
⅛ tsp. garlic salt

Salt and pepper to taste
1 tb. vinegar
¼ cup mayonnaise

Combine sour cream, cheese and garlic salt and blend together. Add salt, pepper and vinegar and blend again. Carefully fold in mayonnaise and blend very briefly so that dressing won't separate. Refrigerate. Makes a little less than one pint.

NOTE: This dressing will keep as long as two weeks if not allowed to stand around out of the refrigerator.

Greek Salad Dressing

½ cup vinegar
1 cup olive oil
1½ tsps. Worcestershire
sauce
1 tsp. sugar

2 cloves garlic, chopped fine
1 tsp. oregano
Salt and pepper to taste

Mix all ingredients in a large jar. Cover and shake well. Let stand for two days at room temperature. Shake well before using. This amount of dressing should suffice for one generous salad large enough for four or five hearty eaters. Larger amounts of dressing can be made by increasing all ingredients proportionately and refrigerating in screw-top jar.

Carrots Arabian

(The name of the landlady in one of the many "Mrs. Murphy's boarding houses" where I stayed in the good old days was not Mrs. Murphy at all. It was Mrs. Fisel, who was from somewhere in the Middle East, and these creamed carrots were one of her many specialties.)

1 bunch carrots, scraped, rinsed and sliced
2 tbs. butter
½ tsp. nutmeg
½ tsp. brown sugar

¼ pint sour cream
1 egg yolk, beaten
1 tb. chopped parsley
Salt and pepper to taste
Chopped chives for garnish

In just enough water to cover, boil carrots until crunchy tender. Set aside in colander to drain. Combine butter, nutmeg and brown sugar. Place carrots in mixing bowl and stir in the butter mixture. When well mixed, stir in the cream and then the egg yolk and parsley. Season to taste and chill in refrigerator until you're ready to serve. Transfer to serving dish and garnish with chives. Serves 4 to 6.

Baked Garbanzos (Chick-Peas)

2 No. 2 cans garbanzos (chick-peas)
2 large very ripe tomatoes
1 large onion, chopped fine
2 cloves garlic, chopped fine

1 tb. tomato paste
¾ cup olive oil
½ tsp. oregano

Spread garbanzos over bottom of baking pan and set aside. Peel tomatoes (dip them quickly in very hot water to facilitate peeling). Then chop fine, combine with remaining ingredients and spread over garbanzos. Preheat oven to 475°F. and bake 40 minutes. Transfer to serving dish. Serves 6.

New Green Beans

2 lbs. fresh string beans
2 tbs. butter
½ tb. bacon drippings
3 cups chicken bouillon
1 tb. flour
1 tsp. sugar

1 tsp. salt
2 tbs. cider vinegar
1 small piece summer savory, optional
1 tb. chopped parsley

Wash beans, break off tips, remove strings and break into about 4 pieces each. Melt butter and bacon drippings in saucepan. Add beans and bouillon, cover and cook about 25 minutes at medium heat or until crisply tender. Test once or twice with fork to make sure they don't overcook, adding more bouillon if necessary. Mix flour, sugar, salt and vinegar and sprinkle over beans. Cook, uncovered, another 2 or 3 minutes. Remove to serving dish, sprinkle with savory and parsley. Serves 6.

New Lima Beans in Cream

1 quart young lima beans, shelled	1 cup heavy cream
2 slices bacon	1½ tbs. lemon juice
1 tsp. salt	1 tb. minced parsley

Wash and drain beans. Place in pot and barely cover with boiling water. Cook at a rapid boil for 15 minutes. Meantime, fry bacon until crisp, drain, crumble and set aside. After beans have boiled 15 minutes, add salt, increase heat and cook until most of water evaporates. Then reduce heat, add cream and bacon, stir in lemon juice and parsley and blend until smooth, taking care not to let boil. Serve steaming hot. Serves 4.

Jake's Potato Pancakes

6 medium potatoes	¼ tsp. grated nutmeg
1 large onion, grated	2 tbs. minced parsley
2 tbs. flour	4 tbs. butter
2 eggs, beaten	2 tbs. bacon drippings (*or*
1½ tsps. salt	1 more tb. butter)
¼ tsp. pepper	

Wash and peel potatoes. Cover with cold water and let stand 30 minutes to crispen. Drain, dry and grate at once. Press out as much liquid as possible and stir in the grated onion. Add flour, eggs, salt, pepper, nutmeg and parsley and stir until well blended. Melt butter and bacon drippings in frying pan until it starts to sizzle. Then gently drop large spoonfuls of the potato mixture into hot fat, 3 or 4 at a time. Fry at high heat, keeping flame just low enough to prevent smoking, until crispy brown on both sides. Remove to hot platter and serve either with sauerbraten at dinner or with bacon at breakfast. Serves 6.

NOTE: Applesauce is a fitting companion no matter what the meal.

Fried Apples and Onions

6 large tart apples	1 tsp. salt
1 tb. butter	½ tsp. paprika
1 tb. bacon drippings	½ cup sugar
2 large onions, sliced	

Wash and core apples but do not peel. Cut into thick slices. Melt butter and bacon fat in frying pan. Make a layer of onion slices in the pan and cook slowly on low heat for 5 minutes. Do not turn. Season with half the salt and all of the paprika, and top with layer of apple slices. Mix remaining salt with the sugar and sprinkle over the apple layer. Increase heat to medium, cover and cook until it starts to steam. Lower heat and cook 2 minutes more. Remove lid, add a bit of butter or hot water if needed, and cook with another 2 minutes. It's delicious, particularly as a side dish with pork but even all by itself as a light-lunch main course. Serves 6.

Lola's Tunaville Jolly Blue Salad

Crisp lettuce leaves	1 1-lb. can blueberries
2 7-oz. cans tuna fish, drained	2 cucumbers, scrubbed clean but unpeeled and sliced thin
1 lb. pot cheese	

Spread lettuce leaves on serving platter. Combine contents of tuna cans into any shape desired in center of lettuce bed. In a separate bowl, combine pot cheese and undrained blueberries; shape this mixture into a ring around the tuna. Lean the unpeeled cucumber slices around the blueberry-pot-cheese ring. Serves 4.

VARIATIONS: Raspberries, strawberries, pineapple, applesauce or just about any fruit (or any combination thereof) can be substituted for the blueberries. Of course, the fruit must be small enough or able to be cut or crushed fine enough for easy mixing. Also, cottage cheese can be substituted for pot cheese.

German Hot Potato Salad

8 slices bacon
3 tbs. flour
4 tsps. onion or scallion, chopped
⅔ cup vinegar, preferably a red wine vinegar
⅔ cup water
½ cup sugar
4 tsps. salt
½ tsp. black pepper, freshly ground
1 tsp. powdered dry mustard

½ tsp. rosemary leaves, crumbled in the palm of your hand
½ clove garlic, finely chopped (optional)
2 quarts potatoes, boiled and diced
½ cup fresh (preferably Italian) parsley, finely minced

Fry bacon until crisp. Remove from pan, drain and crumble. Stir flour and onion or scallion into bacon fat left in pan. Then stir in vinegar, water, sugar, salt, pepper, mustard, rosemary and garlic. Cook until mixture is of medium thickness, stirring gently but constantly. Add potatoes, parsley and crumbled bacon. Mix carefully to prevent mashing. Remove to serving bowl and, if desired, garnish with paprika. Serves 8 to 10.

83

NOTE : The flavor is at its best when served hot, but this potato salad also is excellent when chilled and eaten cold.

Mestika Jim's Braised Celery

12 tender stalks green celery	½ tsp. salt
	¾ tsp. pepper
1½ cups beef soup stock (canned is fine) or bouillon	2 tbs. butter
	½ tsp. flour
	Paprika for garnish

Wash celery, remove all leaves, peel away the tough outside layer and cut into 3-inch lengths. Bring soup stock to a boil in a small pot. Add celery, salt and pepper and simmer until tender, about 10 minutes. Remove celery with slotted ladle, reserve stock and set both aside. Melt butter in large skillet, add flour and stir until brown. Add stock and stir until mixture comes to a boil. Then add celery and simmer about 7 minutes to reduce liquid. Remove celery to serving dish with slotted spoon; garnish with paprika. Serves 4.

Potatoes Au Gratin

4 tbs. butter	1 tsp. brandy
1½ cups finely chopped onions	Salt and pepper to taste
	1 cup cheese dressing, preferably Durkee's
4 cups boiled potatoes, diced	1 cup grated Kraft's Old English cheese
1 tb. Worcestershire sauce	

Melt butter in heavy iron skillet. Add onions and sauté on low heat for 3–4 minutes. Meanwhile, combine potatoes with Worcestershire sauce, brandy, salt and pepper. When onions are tender and translucent, gently stir in the potatoes, pour the cheese dressing over them, cover and continue cooking over low heat until dressing works to the bottom (about 6–8 minutes). Then transfer to well-greased casserole dish, top with the grated cheese and bake on topmost shelf of preheated 350°F. oven until cheese melts and browns about 25–30 minutes). Serves 6.

N O T E : Grated Swiss cheese makes a worthy substitute for the Old English.

Fish and Green Grape Salad

½ to 1 lb. cooked white-meat fish, boned and flaked

2 or 3 stalks tender celery, diced

1 small firm cucumber, peeled and diced

1 small sweet cucumber pickle, diced

4 ripe black olives, sliced

2 cups very ripe seedless green grapes, stems removed

½ to 1 cup mayonnaise

2–4 crisp lettuce leaves

Combine all ingredients except lettuce. Mix well, chill and serve in mounds on lettuce. Serves 2 to 4.

Inez Morris' Chicken-Beef-Noodle Soup

(There is a gal who shares a co-author with me . . . Inez Morris who with husband Dan wrote *The Penny Saver Cookbook*. I am indebted to Inez for this amazingly simple and delightfully tasty recipe—an unusual broth and quick-as-a-flash noodles that go with it. Hardly anyone makes noodles these days, but try these once and I wager you'll make them many more times.)

2 2½-lb. whole chickens, cleaned and washed	3 tender young carrots, washed but unpeeled
2 quarts cold water	1 pinch garlic powder
1 cup beef broth*	¼ tsp. dill weed, dried
2 medium onions, whole	1 tb. salt or to taste
2 medium stalks celery	Noodles

Combine all ingredients in a large, heavy pot. Simmer, covered, for ¾ hour or until broth develops strength you like. Remove chickens and vegetables and strain soup. Let it stand about 10 minutes. Then skim fat off top. Reheat soup to boiling while preparing easy noodles (recipe follows). Serves 6 to 8.

Quick-as-a-Flash Soup Noodles

1 egg	1 pinch salt
1 tb. flour	

Beat egg lightly using hand egg beater. Add flour and salt and beat together with fork. Dump all at once into broth that is boiling briskly but not hard. Boil for about 5 minutes. Gently stir a few times if noodles run together. Serve at once. Makes enough noodles for 1 to 1½ quarts of thin broth—about what recipe above yields.

---

* You can use canned broth if you like, but for a really interesting and different flavor, do it Inez' way. After broiling a steak, she saves, freezes and labels every teaspoonful of delicious sauce that runs through to the dripping pan. Then, when making this chicken broth, she lifts the solidified fat from the tops of some of her little bundles of frozen flavor. (The fat goes into the refrigerator to be used to grease omelet pans.) She mixes enough of the jellied sauce with warm water to give her one cup of nice rich beef broth.

Cab Calloway's Bouillabaisse

2 1¾-lb. cans tomatoes
4 cups water
1 large onion, chopped
1 clove garlic, minced
¼ cup olive (or peanut) oil
1 tsp. salt
¼ tsp. pepper
1 bay leaf
½ tsp. monosodium gluta-
mate
¼ tsp. dried thyme
½ tsp. saffron shreds
2 to 3 lbs. mixed fish, bones
removed, cut in chunks*
4 frozen lobster tails,
thawed overnight in
refrigerator, deveined,
shell left on and cut in
half lengthwise

1 dozen medium or 2
dozen small hardshell
clams, thoroughly
scrubbed and purged of
sand
8 to 10 medium mussels in
the shell, thoroughly
scrubbed and beardlike
appendages on outside of
shell cut away
½ lb. scallops
1 7-oz. can shrimp, drained
½ lb. crab meat, canned or
fresh (if fresh, scrub
claws and include)

Put first 10 ingredients in a large pot, bring to a low boil and cook for 20 minutes. (This part of preparation can be done the night before and mixture stored in refrigerator. Put on stove and bring to a boil before adding other ingredients.) Add saffron to boiling soup and cook 2 or 3 minutes. Stir and add mixed fish chunks and lobster tails. Simmer 10 minutes. Stir and add the remaining ingredients. Simmer very gently for 10 minutes or until all of shells have started to open. Serve in large soup bowls, dividing fish so there is some of everything in each bowl. Thick slabs of French bread go nicely with this dish. Serves 8 to 12.

N O T E : You may prefer to pour off soup and serve it first, then put fish on a preheated platter, using shellfish as a garnish. For a thinner broth, increase amount of water to 6 or 8 cups.

* Bouillabaisse is seldom made just the same way twice in a row. It is a fisherman's soup, and whatever fish is in season is the first to use.

The Lambs' Chicken Gumbo Soup

2 cups stewed tomatoes
⅛ lb. butter
½ cup celery, chopped
½ cup onions, diced
½ cup green peppers, diced

2 small, fresh mushrooms, diced
6 cups chicken stock
1 medium-size fresh okra
Salt and pepper to taste

Drain stewed tomatoes. Set liquid aside and chop tomatoes. Put butter in bottom of large, heavy saucepan and heat until butter melts. Add tomatoes, celery, onions, green peppers and mushrooms. Sauté for 10 minutes. Add juice from stewed tomatoes, chicken stock and okra. Bring to a boil, turn down heat, cover and simmer for 50 minutes. Add salt and pepper to taste and serve. Serves 8.

Louis and Lucille Armstrong's Creole Red Beans with Rice

1 lb. kidney beans, washed
½ lb. salt pork (or substitute 6 small ham hocks or one smoked pork butt)
2 medium onions, diced

¼ green pepper, chopped
5 tiny (or 2 medium) dried peppers
1 clove garlic, chopped
Salt to taste
1 4-oz. can of tomato sauce

Soak beans overnight in cold water to cover. Pour water off beans and put them in 2-quart pot. Add fresh water to cover, add salt pork, cover pot and bring to rapid boil. Turn heat down to slightly higher than low and cook 1½ hours. Add diced onions, chopped green pepper, dried peppers, garlic and salt to taste. Cook for 3 hours at a high simmer. Add tomato sauce and continue cooking for 1½ hours more, adding water whenever necessary. Beans and

ABOVE. Jim and Mary Ameche pose for the camera. But it's only a pose . . .
because Jim seldom samples—he's too anxious to eat what's cooking in the pot.
BELOW. The Sterling Family . . . left to right: Beth, Cathy, Barbara (back),
Linda (front), Nancy, Patty, and Susan.

ABOVE. I needn't tell you who this is with me. All you need do is look at the ash trays. BELOW. Chef Stephen Moltemy shows me and Manager Richard C. Woods what's cooking at The Lambs Club.

ABOVE. Senator Ford (left) and Harry Hershfield serve anecdotes with every course when we lunch at The Lambs Club. RIGHT. Cab Calloway and I come smiling through—perhaps because we've just exchanged some good recipes.

ABOVE. Anthony Pedretti, the "21" Club's fine chef, gives me and mine host, Bob Kriendler, a preview of one of his culinary creations. BELOW. Papa Paul Buzzalino, better known as Gigi, Mama Rose, and son Angelo (Buzzy) of the Rose Restaurant let me know they are serious about their cooking.

This is the best way I know how to say thank you to Louis Armstrong for his contribution to this book.

ABOVE. Jane DeFreitas halts in her cake-baking just long enough to look at the birdie with husband Dick. LEFT. Mike Prelee can't wait for the photographer to leave so that he can dig into wife Carmen's baked meat balls smothered, natch, in spaghetti sauce.

LEFT. As much at home in the kitchen as on the drums . . . that's us, Jack Sterling and Lionel Hampton. BELOW. Yours truly Jack Sterling, otherwise known . . . as the lettering on the hat will attest . . . as "the world's greatest chef," gives host Bill Chan and chef Richard Yee a sampling of Chinese culinary creativity a la the New Gold Coin Restaurant.

ABOVE. My favorite writer of book introductions, Ed Sullivan, and his favorite continental chef, Robert Milanesi, of Umberto's, talk of our favorite subject— food. BELOW. Good cooks like Marcel Haentzler of New York's Americana Hotel receive international recognition of their skills. Chef Haentzler, wearing one of his awards in medallion form, points out a few of his framed diplomas and certificates of award to Bob Tisch and me.

meat should always be just covered with juice, never dry. Serve over or alongside rice (recipe follows). Serves 6 to 8.

TO PREPARE HAM HOCKS OR PORK BUTT (IF SUBSTITUTED FOR SALT PORK)

Wash meat, put in pot, add water to cover and bring to boil over medium flame. Simmer for 1½ hours, then add beans and other ingredients (no salt pork, of course) and continue as above. Simmer for 4½ hours. Add water when necessary.

N O T E : Non-pork eaters may substitute corned beef or beef tongue for the salt pork, ham hocks, or butts.

RICE

2 **cups white rice**   1 **tsp. salt**
3 **cups water**

Wash rice thoroughly. Put water in a pot, bring to a boil, add salt and rice and continue boiling until water is almost evaporated. Cover and turn flame down low. Cook until rice is grainy. Serves 6 to 8.

MEATS

Marinades for Steaks

Because just about everyone is a steak-eater, I think some facts about marinades are in order before referring to the recipes.

Every meat-eater who likes to eat and likes to cook has devised, I'm sure, a marinade that he considers good and which, because he likes it, is good. I've run into literally hundreds of marinade recipes in my lifetime—so many that I can't remember them all—and 98 percent of them are extremely tasty. Below are several of them, and if you never try a single one as given but use them instead as guides to marinades of your own making, I'll consider these few paragraphs worthwhile.

The quantities given in each are for roughly two pounds of meat —and the meat doesn't have to be beef. Try these marinades on lamb or pork, and on poultry, too. And either indoors or out. The source of heat has nothing to do with the marinade. They're good in a kitchen broiler, over a patio barbecue pit, on a backyard charcoal grill or over a campfire.

Eight to twelve hours of marinating in a refrigerator is best, but one or two hours at room temperature will do. The longer the better. To make the marinades, simply mix all of the ingredients together and then let the meat bathe in them, either in bowls deep enough to saturate or in shallow pans, with frequent brushings. When ready to cook, pat the meat almost dry with lint-free cloth towels.

First, the simplest marinade of all . . . one can of beer!

Okay, now the more glamorous ones:

SIMPLE WINE MARINADES: place meat in smallest possible pan or casserole that will permit your meat to lie flat. Pour 2 tbs. of any wine that you desire over meat. Brush both sides to fully cover, and turn and brush often while marinating. Sherry and red wines are best.

ROSÉ WINE: 1½ cups rosé wine, 2 cloves crushed garlic, 2 tsps. salt, 2 tsps. pepper, ½ tsp. rosemary.

KOREAN: 1 tb. sesame oil, ½ tsp. monosodium glutamate, 1 clove crushed garlic, 2 tbs. diced green onion (scallion), 3 tbs. ground sesame seed, 2 tbs. sugar, ⅛ cup soy sauce.

JAPANESE: ⅛ cup soy sauce, 2 tbs. honey, ⅛ tsp. monosodium glutamate, 1 clove minced garlic, ⅛ tsp. ginger.

GREEK: juice of 1 lemon, 1 clove minced garlic, ½ tsp. salt, ¼ tsp. olive oil, ½ tsp. thyme, 1 tsp. black pepper, 2 tbs. chopped onion.

ARTHUR LEM'S HONG KONG MARINADE: 1 cup soy sauce, 1 tsp. sugar, ½ tsp. salt, dash pepper, 1 tsp. ginger juice*, ½ tsp. monosodium glutamate, 1 tsp. minced garlic, 2 tbs. peanut oil.

Pork Ribs in Onion Sauce

3 lbs. spare ribs, cut up	¼ cup chili sauce
1 tb. bacon drippings	3 tbs. lemon juice
3 cups thinly sliced onion	2 tbs. Worcestershire sauce
2 cloves garlic, crushed	3½ tbs. brown sugar
½ cup water	1½ tsps. salt
½ cup vinegar	1 tsp. dry mustard

Preheat oven to 450°F. Place ribs in shallow baking pan and bake for 30 minutes, adding slight amounts of water if necessary (but it shouldn't be). Meantime, melt bacon drippings in heavy pot, add onion and garlic, and sauté until just tender. Add all other ingredients, reduce heat and simmer 10 minutes. Keep warm. When 30 minutes are up, brush ribs with the sauce, reduce oven temperature to 350°F. and bake 1 hour more or until done, brushing about every 10 minutes with the sauce. Place ribs on hot serving platter and top with remaining onion sauce. Serves 6.

* Chinese ginger juice is available in specialty food shops and in shops specializing in Chinese foods.

Twin Meat Logs

1 lb. ground beef	2 tbs. Worcestershire sauce
½ lb. ground pork	4 slices white bread, cubed
½ lb. ground veal	1 cup warm milk
½ cup chopped onion	2 eggs
3 tbs. finely chopped celery	½ cup (about) dry bread
2 tsps. salt	crumbs
¼ tsp. pepper	½ cup chili sauce
½ tsp. sage	4 strips bacon
¼ tsp. dry mustard	½ cup boiling water

Thoroughly mix beef, pork, veal, onion and celery in large bowl. Stir in salt, pepper, sage, mustard, and Worcestershire. Set aside. Soak bread cubes in milk for a couple of minutes, add eggs, beat thoroughly with a whisk (or a rotary beater), add to bowl containing meat and mix. Divide mixture in half, shape into logs and roll each in bread crumbs. Place in a well-greased, shallow baking pan. Spread ¼ cup chili sauce over each log, top each with 2 strips bacon, pour boiling water into pan and bake in 350°F. oven for 1 hour. Serves 8 to 10.

The Aschettino Family's Veal Scaloppine

(In Long Beach, Long Island, New York, there is an old established Italian-family restaurant that goes by the very un-Italian name of Paddy's. The kitchen majordomo is Papa Aschettino who, at 83, tends every dish with Old World know-how. Out front are his twin son and daughter, Lee and Ronnie. Lee is a fine cook like his father, and Ronnie's a stickler for detail like her mother, who still pops in now and then. This is their recipe for veal scaloppine . . . a recipe that Papa got from his Papa, who ran a restaurant in Italy.)

3 lbs. veal steak, ¼ to
⅓ inch thick and then
pounded paper-thin and
cut into 8 serving pieces
½ cup enriched flour
1 tsp. salt
Dash of pepper
2 tsps. paprika
4 tbs. olive oil

1 6-oz. can sliced mush-
rooms
1 beef bouillon cube
1 8-oz. can tomato sauce
¼ cup chopped green pep-
per
1 8-oz. pkg. noodles
Parmesan cheese to taste

Dust pieces of veal in mixture of flour, salt, pepper and paprika. Heat 3 tbs. olive oil in skillet, add veal and brown. Place pieces in baking pan 13 × 9 × 2 inches. Separate mushrooms from their liquid and add water to the liquid to make 1 cup. Bring to a boil, add bouillon cube, stir until dissolved and pour over the browned veal. Place in 350°F. oven and bake 30 minutes. Meanwhile, combine mushrooms, tomato sauce and green pepper and, when 30 minutes are up, sprinkle over the veal and bake another 15 minutes. At the same time, cook noodles according to package directions but adding remaining 1 tb. olive oil to the salted water to prevent sticking. Drain noodles, spread over serving platter, top with veal, pour sauce from pan over all and serve with Parmesan cheese on the side for each to use as desired. Serves 8.

N O T E : Have your butcher pound the veal for you. But, if you must do it yourself, first place the pieces between sheets of waxed paper to make the chore easier.

Veal Shanks with Apple

2 tsps. flour
1 tsp. salt or to taste
⅛ tsp. black pepper or to
taste

6 veal shanks
2 tsps. oil
2 cups cranapple juice
1 or 2 red apples

Combine flour, salt and pepper into a seasoning mixture and use it to dust the veal shanks on all sides. Bring oil to a sizzle in frying pan, add shanks and brown on all sides. Turn oven to 300°F. and while it is preheating, arrange shanks side by side but not touching in baking pan with about 2-inch sides. Pour cranapple juice into pan, cover tightly with aluminum foil, slide into oven and cook for 1 hour. Then remove foil, turn shanks and continue cooking 1 hour more, adding slight amounts of water to pan if needed, or until tops of shanks crispen nicely. Meanwhile, core and cut apple into ¼-inch to ½-inch slices and arrange around shanks during last half-hour. Serves 6.

Veal Medallions with Tarragon

(*Medaillons de Veau à l'estragon*)

(Veal is a staple with gourmet cooks, and this recipe of Chef Haentzler's brings out the best in this delectable meat. If your butcher cannot supply medallions of veal, substitute veal chops.)

2 tbs. butter	Salt and pepper
3 tbs. olive oil	½ cup veal gravy
6 medallions of veal (or	2 branches fresh tarragon
veal chops)	2 tbs. butter

Heat butter with oil and brown veal on both sides. Season with salt and pepper and cook gently for 10 to 12 minutes more. Remove veal and keep hot between two heated plates. Pour off butter-and-oil mixture and reserve; add wine and cook until reduced by two thirds. Add veal gravy, cook to reduce a little and remove from heat. Put the veal back into the sauce, sprinkle with chopped branch of tarragon, cover, and simmer for five minutes. Remove veal and arrange on a heated round plate; blanch tarragon branch in boiling water, and decorate each medallion of veal with a leaf or two. Add butter to the sauce, taste and adjust seasoning. Pour sauce over veal and serve. Serves 6.

Veal Roll-Ups

6 ¼-inch-thick veal cutlets, pounded paper-thin
Fresh ground black pepper to taste
3 thin slices boiled ham, cut in two
½ cup shredded sharp processed American or English cheese
¼ cup chopped stuffed green olives
3 tbs. butter
¼ cup sherry

Sprinkle each cutlet with pepper. Place 1 piece of ham on each. Mix cheese and chopped olives, and spread over the ham. Roll and secure with wooden toothpicks or tie with light wire. Melt butter in skillet, add veal rolls and cook uncovered 25 minutes over low heat, turning occasionally to prevent sticking. Pour sherry over the veal rolls and cook 5 minutes longer. Serves 6.

Rotisserie-Roasted Ham

1 whole ham, 8 to 10 lbs.
¾ cup brown sugar
½ cup unsweetened pine-apple juice
1½ tbs. prepared mustard
A bit more than ¼ cup vin-egar

Remove casing and skin from ham; discard. Score ham and center lengthwise on rotisserie spit and begin roasting. Since cooking time will vary depending upon size and shape of your ham and whether you are cooking over electric coils or charcoal, it's best to use a meat thermometer to tell when done. A cooked or ready-to-eat ham needs an internal temperature of 130°F.; uncooked ham is done at 160°F.

While ham is roasting, prepare a glaze by combining all other ingredients in a pot and simmering, uncovered, for about 10 minutes. About 30 minutes before ham is done brush well with the glaze and repeat the basting process 2 or 3 times in the remaining minutes. When done, place leftover glaze on table in a gravy dish for those who want more on their ham. This size ham will serve about 12 people and leave plenty for ham and eggs and sandwiches the next day.

Mr. Parris's Marinated Lamb Chops

½ cup olive oil
Juice of large lemon
¼ tsp. oregano

6 shoulder lamb chops,
1 inch thick

Thoroughly mix olive oil, lemon juice and oregano. Place chops side by side on shallow baking pan. Pour half of marinade on one side, turn and repeat. Let stand at least 2 hours, turning several times and brushing occasionally if necessary to make sure the meat is thoroughly covered. Wipe or pat almost dry with lint-free towel. Preheat broiler to 500°F., transfer chops to broiler rack 3 inches from heat and broil as you like them. Figure about 6 minutes on each side for medium. Meantime, pour leftover marinade, if any, into small pot and pour a bit on each chop when serving. Serves 6.

N O T E : This recipe does mighty well on a charcoal grill, too.

Chili Con Carne and Chili Mac

2 tbs. shortening, preferably suet
1 lb. ground beef
1 cup chopped onion
½ tsp. salt
½ tsp. garlic, minced
1 tsp. paprika
1 cup tomato sauce

1 beef bouillon cube dis-
solved in ½ cup water
2½ tsps. chili powder dissolved in 2 tsps. water
2 cups canned kidney
beans, drained
¾ pkg. spaghettini

Melt shortening in chafing dish or heavy pot. Stir in ground beef and cook until browned. Add onion and cook until yellow. Mix in remaining ingredients, except spaghettini, and cook gently about 30 minutes or until meat is tender and sauce is cooked down. Meanwhile, prepare spaghettini according to package directions. To serve, heap pasta on plates; top with generous amounts of chili. Serves 6.

VARIATION: Rice may be substituted for the pasta.

NOTE: The recipe, as given, is for Chili Mac. Serve it without either spaghettini or rice and you have Chili Con Carne.

Mexican Beef Steak

½ cup flour
1 tsp. salt
⅛ tsp. pepper
1½ lbs. top round steak, cut ½ inch thick
⅓ cup oil
1 clove garlic, minced
1 large red onion, thinly sliced

½ green pepper, thinly sliced
2 cups canned tomatoes
6 pickled peppers
⅓ cup stuffed green olives
Tomato juice, if needed

Combine flour, salt and pepper and rub into both sides of steak. Heat oil in heavy pot, add garlic, onion and green pepper and cook until they begin to wilt. Remove with slotted spoon. Add steak to the pot and sauté until deep brown on both sides. Lower heat, return the cooked onion-garlic-pepper mixture to the pot along with the canned tomatoes and leftover seasoned flour. Cover and cook very slowly about 1 to 1½ hours or until steak is tender. Add pickled peppers and olives. If the pot juices are too thick, add some tomato juice. Stir, cook another 3 or 4 minutes, and serve. Serves 6.

Spanish Boiled Dinner

Cocido (Boiled meat and vegetables)

1 fricasee chicken, cut up
6 quarts water
Salt and pepper to taste
2 cups dried garbanzos (chick-peas), soaked overnight in salt water
6 links Spanish sausage or, if unavailable, mild Italian
½ lb. salt pork
2 lbs. lamb shoulder

¾ lb. ground beef
¾ lb. ground pork
2 eggs, beaten
½ cup bread crumbs
2 tbs. flour
6 potatoes, peeled and quartered
1 bunch carrots, sliced
1 medium cabbage, cut in wedges

Wash chicken. Place in large pot, cover with cold water, add salt and pepper. Boil 10 minutes. Then reduce heat and simmer for another 30 minutes. Skim fat off surface and add drained garbanzos, sausage, salt pork and lamb and continue simmering. Combine ground beef, ground pork, eggs, bread crumbs, flour, salt and pepper. Mix well and shape into a large ball. Place on top of chicken, pork and lamb in pot. Cook 30 minutes. Add potatoes, carrots and cabbage and give the entire stew a final 30 minutes of cooking. Serve spoonfuls of meat mixture with spoonfuls of other ingredients and liquid. Serves 10 to 12.

Sausage and Cheese Loaf

2 lbs. Italian sausage, mild or hot to taste
2 eggs
½ lb. cheddar cheese, diced, sharp or mild to taste

1 cup cracker crumbs
½ cup milk
½ cup chopped onion

Remove sausage from casing and place meat in mixing bowl. Beat eggs well, add to sausage along with all other ingredients and mix well. Thoroughly grease casserole (about 9 × 5 × 3), add mixture and bake 1 hour in 325°F. oven. Serves 6 to 8.

Mrs. Hamerschlag's Sauerbraten (*Marinated Beef*)

1 4-lb. pot roast, rump, chuck or round	1 tsp. salt
	1 tsp. whole peppercorns
12 juniper berries, crushed	1 tsp. whole allspice
2 cups cider vinegar	2 tsps. horseradish
2 quarts beer	½ tsp. ground ginger
1 cup sugar	

Place beef in deep glass bowl. Combine all other ingredients and pour over meat. Cover and store in refrigerator for 3 to 5 days, turning each day. Remove meat, pat dry with paper towels and place in roasting pot. Strain marinade, pour about 2 cups over meat, cover and simmer about 1½ hours or until tender. Serve with potato dumplings (recipe follows). Serves 6 to 8.

N O T E : Sauerbraten with potato dumplings is a marriage made in culinary heaven. Mrs. Hamerschlag's recipe follows.

Mrs. Hamerschlag's Potato Dumplings (*Kartoffelklosse*)

2 eggs	¼ tsp. salt
6 medium potatoes, cooked and mashed	2 tbs. butter
	2 tbs. bread crumbs
¼ cup flour	

Beat the eggs into the mashed potatoes, then the flour and salt. Shape into balls and poach about 10 minutes in gently boiling salt water. Meanwhile, melt butter in skillet and stir in bread crumbs until brown. Roll dumplings in browned crumbs and serve immediately with sauerbraten.

Jake's Kenosha Sauerbraten

3 lbs. round steak	1 pint red wine vinegar
1 tb. salt	2 bay leaves
½ tsp. pepper	2 tbs. beef suet
2 onions, sliced	6 tbs. butter
1 carrot, sliced	5 tbs. flour
1 stalk celery, chopped	1 tb. sugar
4 cloves	10 ginger snaps, crushed
4 peppercorns	

Wipe steak with damp cloth. Mix salt and pepper and rub over surface. Place in nonmetallic bowl, preferably earthenware. Combine onions, carrot, celery, cloves, peppercorns, vinegar and bay leaves and pour over meat. Cover bowl and marinate in refrigerator for 4 days. On fifth day remove and drain. Melt suet in large heavy pot. Add meat and sauté lightly on both sides. Add 1 tb. butter and sear well on both sides. Add marinade liquid and bring to a boil. Lower heat and simmer 3 hours. Melt 5 tbs. butter in separate pan, stir flour into it well, add sugar, stir, and let brown until it's a smooth dark mixture. Add to meat. Cover and continue cooking until tender, about 1 hour more. Remove meat to warm platter. Stir crushed ginger snaps into pot juices until thick, then pour over meat. Serve at once. Serves 6.

N O T E : Potato dumplings or pancakes, along with a full-bodied red wine, are perfect companions for sauerbraten.

Barbecued Spareribs

2 large onions, sliced	½ tsp. black pepper
4 lbs. spareribs, cut in about 4 1-lb. pieces	1 cup catsup
	1 cup water
2 tbs. steak sauce	½ tsp. red pepper
1 tsp. paprika	½ tsp. chili powder
1 tb. salt	

Line bottom of baking pan with onion slices and top with spareribs. Combine all other ingredients and pour over ribs. Bake in 325°F. oven 3 hours, adding water from time to time if necessary. Serves 4.

Barbecued Frankfurters

8 frankfurters	1 tsp. minced chives
1 or 2 tbs. butter	1 tsp. mixed fresh herbs
2 cups tomato sauce	¼ tsp. garlic powder, or
1 tb. pickle relish	less but no more
1 tb. chopped onion	½ tsp. sugar
1 tsp. minced parsley	½ to ¾ tsp. Worcestershire
4 cloves	sauce, to taste

Slit frankfurters. Melt butter in chafing dish or heavy skillet, add franks and turn often until slightly browned. Combine all other ingredients in bowl, pour over franks, stir and cook until sauce is steaming but not boiling. Serves 4 or 8, depending on appetites.

NOTE: These barbecued franks are delicious served on beds of rice or with mashed potatoes. Raisin muffins also go well. Or serve them the way kids like them best, on hot-dog buns with the sauce spooned on like mustard.

Midwest Steak with Onions

4 slices bacon	⅛ to ¼ cup flour
6 small onions, sliced	¼ tsp. garlic powder
2 lbs. steak, pounded well and cut into strips ½ inch thick	Salt and pepper to taste
	Boiling water

Set chafing dish pan over direct heat. When good and hot, add bacon and cook until brown. Remove bacon, add onion slices and cook in bacon grease until tender. Remove about ⅔ of the onion, place steak strips on onion remaining in pan and cover with remaining onion. Dredge thickly with flour, season with garlic powder, salt and pepper. Add just enough boiling water to barely cover the steak. Place lid on pan and cook 30 to 40 minutes or until steak is tender. Serves 2 to 4.

N O T E : A heavy skillet may be substituted for the chafing dish.

Wiener Schnitzel

1 egg	3 tbs. butter
½ cup cracker crumbs	1 lemon, sliced
1 tsp. salt	8 anchovy fillets
½ tsp. pepper	2 tbs. capers
4 ¼-lb. slices of veal	

Break egg into a dish. Mix crumbs, salt and pepper in another dish and then dip veal slices first in egg and then in crumbs until coated on both sides. Melt butter in skillet. Add veal and fry until golden brown on both sides. If gravy is desired, remove meat from skillet and stir ½ cup boiling water into drippings. Pour gravy over veal and garnish with lemon slices, anchovies and capers. Serves 4.

Easy Tamale Pie

2 tbs. oil	1½ tsps. salt
1 onion, chopped	1½ tsps. chili powder
1 lb. ground beef	½ cup ripe olives, pitted
2 cups canned tomatoes	½ lb. Monterey jack cheese
2 cups creamed corn	cut into small chunks
1 cup milk	about ⅛ inch thick
1 cup uncooked yellow cornmeal	

Heat oil in a heavy skillet and sauté the chopped onion until soft. Add beef and sauté until lightly brown, stirring to blend in with the onion. Stir in all remaining ingredients except olives and cheese. Mix well. Add olives, stir, and cover all with chunks of cheese. Cover and cook over low heat 20 to 30 minutes. Serves 6 to 8.

N O T E : Monterey jack cheese is not sharp. If you cannot find it, use sliced yellow American cheese or a mild cheddar. Or, if you like, a sharp cheddar.

Beef with Tomatoes and Peppers

(Ingredients are divided into 2 lists for easier following)

NO. 1

1 tb. oyster sauce
2 drops sesame oil
½ tsp. sugar

½ tsp. monosodium gluta-
mate
Dash of pepper

NO. 2

1½ tbs. oil
¼ tsp. salt
1 small clove garlic
¼ tsp. minced ginger, op-
tional
1½ cups cooked beef, cut
into pieces about ¼ × 3
inches
½ tb. dry sherry wine

1 tsp. dark soy sauce
1 cup beef soup stock
2 large green peppers, cut
into 12 pieces
2 large tomatoes, cut into
12 pieces
2 tbs. cornstarch dissolved
in 1 tb. water

Combine all ingredients in No. 1, stir well and set aside. Heat oil in skillet until it starts to sizzle, add salt, garlic and ginger and brown slightly. Discard garlic and as much of ginger as possible. Add beef and stir 2 minutes. Add sherry and soy sauce, mix well and remove beef from pan. Put soup stock and Mixture No. 1 in pan and stir well until it boils. Return beef to pan, add green peppers and tomatoes and stir 1 minute. Add cornstarch mixture, 1 spoon at a time, and stir to desired consistency. Serves 4.

VARIATIONS: Pork, chicken, veal, shrimp or lobster may replace beef. String beans, snow peas, broccoli or asparagus may replace tomatoes and peppers.

Roast Pork Fried Rice

(Ingredients are divided into 2 lists for easier following)

NO. 1

1 tb. dark soy sauce	½ tsp. sugar
¼ tsp. molasses	½ tsp. monosodium gluta-
1 tb. light soy sauce	mate

NO. 2

1½ tbs. oil	4 cups cooked rice
¼ tsp. salt	¼ cup chopped scrambled
Dash of black pepper	eggs
½ cup chopped onion	1 cup canned bean sprouts,
¾ cup roast pork, cut into	drained
pieces about ⅛ × 2	
inches	

Combine all ingredients listed in No. 1, stir well, and set aside. Preheat skillet and add oil. When it starts to sizzle, add salt, pepper, and onion and stir until onions are translucent. Add roast pork and stir 1 minute. Add rice and mix very well. Now add Mixture No. 1 and keep stirring and tossing until evenly browned, taking care not to let rice burn. Add egg and bean sprouts, stir 1 minute more and serve. Serves 4.

VARIATIONS: Chicken, beef, ham, bacon, shrimp, lobster or crab meat may be used instead of pork. Sliced canned water chestnuts or shredded lettuce may be added with bean sprouts.

Pork Chops with Kumquats and Pineapple

3 tbs. oil
6 pork chops, about
¾ inches thick
Salt and pepper to taste
6 slices pineapple

6 kumquats
½ cup syrup from pine-
apple can
½ cup water

Heat oil in skillet. Add chops and brown on both sides. Season with salt and pepper. Place 1 pineapple slice on each chop and place 1 kumquat in center of each. Combine pineapple syrup and water, pour into skillet, cover tightly and simmer from 45 to 60 minutes or until done, checking occasionally to move and prevent sticking. Serves 6.

NOTE: If you like, try adding a few drops of soy sauce to the water-and-syrup mixture. Or omit soy sauce from the mixture and sprinkle instead on the chops after fruit is in place.

Leftover Latkas

2½ cups ground leftover
cooked meat (beef, pork,
veal, lamb or what have
you)
1½ cups leftover mashed
potatoes
Salt and pepper to taste

1 tsp. thickened meat
sauce, preferably A-1
Sauce
2 tsps. minced onion
⅛ tsp. garlic powder, op-
tional
Flour to coat
2 tbs. oil

Combine meat, potatoes, seasonings, meat sauce, onion and (if desired) garlic powder. Mix well and shape into cakes. Dust lightly with flour. Add oil to skillet or pancake griddle and, when sizzling hot but not smoking, add cakes and fry until brown on both sides. Serves 6.

N O T E : Just about any leftover cooked vegetable may be substituted for or added to the meat. The ones that go best in our house are spinach, broccoli, cauliflower, mashed turnips and squash.

Beef Stew à la Mulligan

6 tbs. shortening
3 lbs. beef, chuck, round or rump, cut into 1-inch cubes
2 medium onions, coarsely chopped
4 cups water
1 cup red wine
2 beef bouillon cubes
1 clove garlic, finely chopped
2 tbs. parsley, finely chopped
1 bay leaf
⅛ tsp. dry thyme leaves

1½ tsps. salt
¼ tsp. pepper
6 medium potatoes, peeled and quartered
6 medium carrots, peeled and cut into 1- or 2-inch pieces
10 small whole white onions, peeled
4 stalks celery, cut into 1- or 2-inch pieces
2 medium green peppers, cut into 2-inch pieces
2 firm medium tomatoes, quartered

Melt shortening in heavy pot or Dutch oven over medium heat. Add cubed beef, brown well on all sides, remove and set aside. Sauté onions until tender. Return meat to pot, add water, wine, bouillon cubes, garlic, parsley, bay leaf, thyme, salt and pepper. Cover and simmer 1½ hours. Add potatoes, carrots, onions and celery and simmer about 40 minutes more. Add peppers and tomatoes and cook another 20 minutes. Serves 6.

N O T E : If desired, thicken gravy by smoothly blending ¼ cup flour into ¼ cup water and, about 3 minutes before stew is done, stirring into juices in pot or Dutch oven.

Creamed Hungarian Goulash

6 tbs. butter
5 onions, chopped
2 tsps. salt
2 tbs. paprika
½ tsp. pepper

3 lbs. beef (chuck is fine),
cut into 1- to 2-inch cubes
1 8-oz. can tomato sauce
1 clove garlic, sliced fine
½ cup sour cream

Melt 4 tbs. butter in heavy kettle. Add onions and sauté until golden brown, stirring constantly. Remove onions and set aside. Combine salt, paprika and pepper on sheet of wax paper and roll meat cubes in mixture. Melt remaining 2 tbs. butter in kettle. Add meat, a few pieces at a time, and brown well on all sides. Set aside and keep warm. Combine meat with the sautéed onions, tomato sauce, and garlic and stir. Cover kettle and cook over low heat, stirring occasionally, for 3 hours. Add sour cream and stir, making sure the goulash does not come to a boil. Serve over noodles. Serves 6.

Hungarian Goulash

3 tbs. butter or margarine
2¼ tsps. salt
3 cups thinly sliced onions
6 tsps. paprika

1½ lbs. beef (chuck, rump,
or round), cut in 1-inch
cubes
½ tsp. garlic powder
3 cups water (about)

Melt butter or margarine in heavy kettle or Dutch oven. Add salt and onions and sauté until golden. Add 1½ tsps. paprika and meat, mix well, cover and simmer over low heat for 1 hour. Add 4½ tsps. paprika, garlic powder, and water to just cover meat. Replace lid and cook 1 hour more or until tender, adding a bit more water when almost done to provide more gravy if desired. Serve on bed of noodles or with mashed potatoes. Serves 4.

NOTE: Instead of noodles or mashed potatoes, goulash acquires a nicely different flavor if you add quartered raw potatoes to the pot during the last half-hour of cooking.

Filet Mignon in a Bacon Collar

4 steak fillets, 1½ inches   8 slices bacon
thick

Let package of bacon strips stand at room temperature for at least an hour so that they will peel away without tearing. Using 2 bacon strips end to end, wrap around outside edge of fillets to form tight-fitting collars. Secure with wooden toothpicks. Place steaks in preheated broiler 3 inches from source of heat and broil 10 minutes on each side for medium rare. Serves 4.

N O T E : Do not overlap bacon strips in forming collars. If just 1 or 1½ strips will completely circle the steaks, that's fine.

Veal Piccatta

(*Veal in Lemon Sauce, Italian Style*)

1 lb. veal scallops (slices)   2 tbs. butter
¼ cup flour   2 tbs. lemon juice
1½ tsps. salt   2 or 3 drops Worcestershire
¼ tsp. black pepper,   sauce
   freshly ground   2 tbs. Italian parsley, finely
4 tbs. vegetable oil, pref-   minced
   erably one without flavor

Have the butcher pound the veal scallops (slices) until they are no more than ⅛ inch thick. Dip the slices in mixture of flour, salt and pepper. Heat the oil and butter in a large skillet until it sizzles. Add veal slices in a single layer and brown on both sides over a medium flame. When tender (a matter of only a couple of minutes) remove from skillet and pour off all but about a tsp. of the drippings. Add lemon juice, Worcestershire and parsley. Return veal to skillet and move about and turn with fork, still over medium flame, until nicely coated with lemon juice, Worcestershire and parsley mixture (a matter of seconds). Place on hot platter, top with drippings that remain in the skillet and serve immediately. Serves 4.

N O T E : If your skillet is too small, use a second at same time, and dividing the shortenings 2 parts oil to 1 part butter.

Soy Sauce Spiced Beef

2 scallions
2 tbs. peanut oil
1 lb. boneless stewing beef, cut into 1-inch cubes
2 tbs. dry sherry

3 tbs. Kikkoman soy sauce
1 tsp. sugar
1 cup cold water
½ tsp. star anise, or 5 drops of anise extract

Wash scallions and cut into 2-inch pieces, using both white bulbs and the green stems. Heat oil in saucepan over high flame. Add cubes of beef and turn until well seared on all sides. Add dry sherry, soy sauce and sugar. Mix well and cook 2 or 3 minutes. Stir in scallion pieces. Add water and bring to a boil. Reduce flame to medium, cover pan and cook 20 minutes more, stirring occasionally. Then stir in anise, reduce flame to low, cover and cook for another 20 minutes. Serves 4.

N O T E : Star anise is available in most Chinese grocery stores; anise extract is obtainable in drug stores. Soy Sauce Spiced Beef may be served either hot or cold and can be frozen and reheated without thawing.

Arthur Lem's Hong Kong Lamb and Leek

(Lamb and mutton are not popular meats in China—not because they aren't liked but because sheep always have been raised there mainly for wool for clothing and not for food. There are, however, some good Chinese recipes for lamb and this is one of them, given to me by Arthur Lem who, with Dan Morris, wrote the *Hong Kong Cookbook.*)

1 lb. shoulder lamb, sliced ⅛ inch thick and then cut into 1½-inch squares	(remove skin before mincing)
1½ tbs. flour	4 tsps. garlic
¼ tsp. salt	1 quart peanut oil
¼ tsp. pepper	2 tsps. sherry wine
6 leeks	1 cup water
2 tbs. soy sauce	4 cups (about) cooked white rice
1 tsp. vinegar	Shredded lettuce or water-
2 tsps. minced ginger root	cress for garnish

Dust each piece of lamb in a mixture of flour, salt and pepper and set aside. Slice leeks in half lengthwise, separate layers, wash well in cold water, cut diagonally into 2-inch pieces and set aside in colander to drain. Combine soy sauce, vinegar, ginger root and garlic, mix into a well-blended sauce and set aside.

Pour peanut oil into deep fryer and heat to 375°F. Place lamb in deep-fry basket, lower into oil, and cook about 2 minutes, tossing gently, or until nicely brown on all sides. Set aside to drain. (Oil may be strained, poured into jar and saved for another day.) Transfer 3 tbs. of the hot oil to wok* or heavy skillet, add leek and stir-fry over medium heat until leaves turn brown, about 2 minutes. Remove wok or skillet from heat, add browned lamb and sherry and return to high heat. When sherry sizzles, add the sauce and 1 cup of water and simmer until lamb is tender, about 35–45 minutes. Transfer lamb and leek to center of platter, border with a ring of white rice, add color by garnishing lightly with shredded lettuce or watercress. Serves 4.

---

* A wok is an all-purpose metal Chinese cooking pot, shaped to fit the fires of old but still very much in use. It is widely available in America.

Corned Beef Dinner

3 to 4 lbs. corned beef
  brisket
2 large onions, sliced
2 cloves garlic, minced
6 whole cloves
2 bay leaves

6 small potatoes, peeled
6 small carrots, scraped
1 medium cabbage, cut
  into 6 wedges
1 tb. lemon juice

Place corned beef in large pot and add enough hot water to barely cover. Add onions, garlic, cloves and bay leaves, place cover on pot and simmer 1 hour for each pound of meat, or until tender. Remove beef to platter and store in warm oven. Add potatoes and carrots to liquid in pot, cover and boil 10 minutes. Then add cabbage and lemon juice (to stifle those odors to which those theatrical hotels so objected). Cook another 15–20 minutes but no longer, if, like me, you like your cabbage with a bit of a bite to it. Arrange wedges on platter with corned beef, potatoes and carrots and serve. Serves 6 to 8.

Pork Chops Stuffed with Corn

8 double-rib pork chops,
  with pockets cut in by
  butcher
Salt and pepper to taste
1 12-oz. can whole kernel
  corn
2 tbs. chopped pimento
2 tbs. chopped celery

2 tbs. chopped green pep-
  per
¼ cup chopped onion
½ cup bread crumbs
½ tsp. salt
½ tsp. thyme
¼ tsp. sage

Rub inside of pork chop pockets with salt and pepper. Combine all of the remaining ingredients in a bowl, mix well and stuff the mixture into the pockets. Close the pockets by inserting wooden toothpicks or metal skewers through the meat on the fatty edges. Do this on an angle so that the picks or skewers will not keep the chops from lying flat in the pan. Wrap twine around the picks or skewers to close tightly. Lightly grease a heavy skillet. Brown chops slowly on each side and then transfer to well-greased baking pan. Add ½ cup hot water to the skillet drippings, mix well, and pour over the chops. Cover tightly (aluminum foil makes a good cover) and bake in preheated 350°F. oven for 1 hour, basting and adding water as needed. Uncover and bake 30 minutes more. Remove picks or skewers and string and serve. Serves 8.

Ham Cantonese

1 10–12 lb. Virginia ham (no other kind will do)	1 tsp. five-spice powder*
4 ginger roots, peeled, cut up and crushed	3 pieces orange rind, about 1 inch long
2 green onions, cut into 1-inch pieces	6 star anise seeds
1 cup cooking sherry	2 cups soy sauce
18 peppercorns	8 tbs. sugar
	Parsley sprigs for garnish

Place ham in large pot. Add just enough water to cover ginger and onions and bring to a boil over high heat. Add all other ingredients, cover, and simmer about 7 hours or until skin becomes lustrous. Remove to warm platter, garnish with parsley sprigs and serve. Serves 20 with lots left over.

Lamb Chops Baked in Wine

6 shoulder lamb chops, 1 inch thick	1 tb. olive oil
1 clove garlic	1 medium onion, minced
Salt and pepper to taste	1 tb. minced parsley
2 tbs. butter	1½ tbs. flour
	1 cup dry white wine

* Five-spice powder is available in specialty shops selling Chinese foods.

Rub the chops well with garlic and season to taste with salt and pepper. Add butter and oil to large heavy skillet and, when butter melts and mixture starts to sizzle, add chops. Brown well on both sides, about 7 minutes per side. Remove chops to warm dish. Add onion and parsley to skillet and stir, sautéing lightly for about 4–5 minutes. Blend in the flour, and when smooth, slowly stir in the wine. Arrange chops in shallow baking pan, pour wine sauce over them, cover and bake in 375°F. oven for 20 minutes. Remove cover and bake about 10 minutes more or until lightly brown. Serves 6.

The Hotel Roosevelt's Fillet of Beef Wellington

2 lbs. fillet of beef	1 tsp. parsley flakes
2 ozs. butter	6 ozs. imported goose liver
4 pieces shallot (finely chopped)	pâté
	1 cup bread crumbs
6 mushrooms (finely chopped)	Pie dough (your regular recipe for 2-crust pie)
2 ozs. prosciutto or other ham (finely chopped)	1 beaten egg

Have your butcher remove fat from a fillet taken from the center cut. Roast the fillet in a greased pan in a hot oven until lightly browned on all sides. Cooking time should not exceed 7 to 8 minutes. Remove and let cool. Then refrigerate for one hour.

Melt butter in a small saucepan, add the shallots and cook for a few minutes. Add mushrooms and ham. Cook and stir for about 10 minutes. Add parsley and let mixture cool. When almost cold, work in the goose liver until well blended.

Roll out the pie dough. Baste the roasted fillet with the mushroom mixture. Roll in bread crumbs, then wrap in pie dough. Baste dough with beaten egg and bake in a sheet pan in a moderate over for 35 minutes. Let stand 10 minutes before slicing the fillet. Serves 4.

The Hotel Roosevelt's Beef Stroganoff

8 ozs. butter
5 ozs. flour
1 quart milk
Salt to taste
Pinch of cayenne pepper
1 very small bay leaf
1 medium onion (sliced)
1 lb. mushrooms (sliced)
1 cup white wine
6 tbs. tomato paste

1 tb. dry English mustard
1 quart sour cream
5 lbs. fillet of beef (cut in strips about 2½ inches long)
Pepper to taste
½ cup vegetable shortening
Juice of 4 lemons

Melt 5 ozs. butter in a small saucepan. Blend in the flour and cook for 8 to 10 minutes over low heat while stirring constantly. Add 1 quart warm milk, a pinch of salt, a touch of cayenne pepper and bay leaf. Whip the sauce with a whisk and cook for about 20 minutes. Strain and set aside.

Melt 2 ozs. butter in a casserole on top of stove, add the sliced onion and mushrooms, stir until onions are translucent. Add wine and reduce. Stir in the tomato paste and simmer a few minutes. Add the cream sauce and the English mustard diluted with some warm water. Cook for a few minutes. Remove sauce from the fire and blend in the sour cream. Do not allow the sauce to boil. Set aside.

Season the meat with salt and pepper and sauté in a sauté pan with vegetable shortening. Cook over high heat for about 4 or 5 minutes. Pour off the cooking fat and add meat to the prepared sauce. (It is preferable to prepare this dish 15 minutes before serving so as to allow all ingredients to blend together.) Correct seasoning if necessary, and just before serving add the juice of 4 lemons. Serves 10.

NOTE: Rice pilaf and fresh cut string beans are usually served with stroganoff.

Broiled Steak, Greek Style

4 T-bone steaks
Half stick of butter*
Salt and pepper to taste

Juice of 2 lemons
Oregano to taste

Place steaks on broiler pan and dot with one-third of the butter. Mix salt, pepper and lemon juice and sprinkle one-third over the steaks. Sprinkle one side of each steak with a dash of oregano and then broil to your liking on that side, basting 2 or 3 times with pan juices. Turn, dot with another third of butter and a third of lemon juice mixture, sprinkle with oregano and broil second side to your liking, again basting 2 or 3 times. Remove to platter, sprinkle with remaining lemon juice mixture, dot with remaining butter and serve piping hot. Serves 4.

Lamb with Celery and Lemon Sauce

(*Arni Me Selino Avgolemono*)

½ cup butter
2 lbs. lean stewing lamb, cut into 2- or 3-inch pieces
1 large onion, chopped
1 No. 2 can tomatoes

1½ cups hot water
Salt and pepper to taste
1 celery stalk, cut into 1-inch pieces
Lemon Sauce (recipe below)

Melt ¼ cup butter in heavy pot. Add lamb and lightly brown over medium heat (about 5 minutes). Add remaining butter and onions and cook to brown, stirring occasionally, another 10 minutes. Add tomatoes and cook over high heat for 5 minutes more. Then add hot water, salt and pepper, reduce heat to low, cover and cook until meat is tender, about 1½ hours. Add celery and cook another hour. Turn off heat and let stand while preparing Lemon Sauce. Serves 6.

* This amount of butter should do it, but don't hesitate to use more if needed.

LEMON SAUCE

(Avgolemono)

2 eggs   3 tbs. broth in which lamb
½ cup lemon juice   and celery cooked

Beat eggs until light and fluffy. Slowly beat in the lemon juice, also gradually adding the broth as you do so. Add this sauce to pot containing lamb and celery stew, stirring carefully to prevent curdling. Cover and let stand away from heat for 10 minutes before serving.

Grecian Gardens Leg of Lamb

(*Psito Arni*)

1 5- or 6-lb. leg of lamb   1 cup water
Juice of 1 large lemon   24 small potatoes (or quar-
4 garlic cloves, sliced fine   tered pieces of 6 large
Salt and pepper to taste   ones)
¼ cup melted butter

Wipe meat well with damp cloth, pat dry and place in roasting pan. Mix lemon juice, garlic, salt and pepper. Cut several small incisions in leg of lamb, remove as many garlic slices as needed from lemon juice mixture and stuff them into the slashes. Rub the balance of the mixture into the lamb. Pour the melted butter into bottom of pan, cover and roast at 350°F. for 1 hour. Add cup of water to the gravy and continue roasting for 45 minutes. Place potatoes in pan around roast and cook another 45 minutes or until meat is tender and well browned. Baste often throughout. Serves 8.

Mestika Jim's Baked Macaroni and Meat

(This is a four-part recipe that reads harder than it really is. And it's well worth the effort.)

PART ONE

1 6-oz. can tomato paste	2 large onions, chopped
2 cups boiling water	fine
2 tbs. olive oil	1 tsp. cinnamon
2 lbs. chopped beef	Salt and pepper to taste
¼ cup butter	

Blend tomato paste with 1 cup boiling water and set aside. Heat oil in frying pan. When oil starts to sizzle, add chopped meat and sauté over high flame for 15 minutes, stirring often. Then stir in butter and onions and continue to brown 15 minutes more, stirring occasionally. Add tomato paste-and-water mixture, cinnamon, remaining cup of boiling water, salt and pepper to taste. Stir. Cover and cook another 15 minutes over medium flame. Remove lid and cook 10 minutes more to thicken, stirring now and then. Remove from flame and cool. Set aside and prepare . . .

PART TWO

1½ lbs. thin macaroni	cheese (if unavailable,
2 eggs, well beaten	use grated mild cheddar)
1 cup grated Kafaloteri	½ cup butter

Cook macaroni in rapidly boiling salted water for 10 minutes. Remove to colander and drain well, rinsing with cold water to remove excess starch. Place half of macaroni in mixing bowl, add eggs and stir thoroughly. Spread this macaroni over bottom of 11 × 14 baking pan and sprinkle with ½ cup cheese. Spread meat sauce (Part One) over and pat firmly. Place remaining macaroni over meat sauce, sprinkle with remaining cheese. Melt butter and pour over entire surface. Set aside and prepare . . .

PART THREE

(A cream sauce, or as they say in Greece, *Krema Saltsa*)

1 quart milk	4 eggs, well beaten
1 stick butter	Salt to taste
3 heaping tbs. flour	

Heat half the milk with all the butter in large saucepan over medium flame for 7 minutes. While that is cooking, sift flour into remaining milk and stir until smooth. Add eggs to flour-milk mixture and continue stirring until smooth and well blended. When the 7 minutes are up add the mixture to the hot milk, salt to taste and continue cooking 15 minutes more or until it thickens and comes to a boil. Remove from heat immediately, stir well and spread over contents of baking pan. Set aside and prepare . . .

PART FOUR

1 cup grated Kafaloteri cheese (or grated mild cheddar)	2 tsps. cinnamon, or to taste

Combine cinnamon and cheese. Sprinkle over contents of baking pan and now you're set.

Preheat oven to 400°F., slide pan onto rack and join your 15 guests in a slug of Greek brandy (Metaxa) while it bakes for 30 minutes. Then remove from oven, let cool for 15 minutes and cut into 16 squares.

Mrs. Murphy's Pork Chops and Cider Cream Gravy

½ tsp. salt	6 loin pork chops, about
½ tsp. pepper	¾ inch thick
½ tsp. powdered sage	2 cups apple cider

Spread mixture of salt, pepper and sage over both sides of chops and sauté in hot skillet until brown. Reserve fat drippings in skillet and transfer chops to baking pan, side by side but not touching. Add apple cider to pan and bake for about 1 hour in moderate oven preheated to 350°F. Baste occasionally with apple cider from pan, adding more if necessary. Serves 6. Meantime you can be making . . .

Cider Cream Gravy

Fat drippings in skillet	Sauce from baking pan
4 tbs. flour	1½ cups milk

Wait until drippings in skillet have cooled and the fat has solidified. Retain all of the brown meat juice, discard all but approximately 3 tbs. of fat and stir in 4 tbs. flour. When chops are done, pour sauce from pan into a small bowl and skim off all possible fat. Stir remaining sauce into flour mixture in the skillet and add milk. Cook gravy over low heat, stirring constantly until lumps disappear and it thickens. Pour into gravy boat and serve not only with pork chops but also with . . .

Baking Powder Biscuits

2 cups flour	¼ cup vegetable shortening
4 tsps. baking powder	¾ cup milk
½ tsp. salt	
1 tsp. sugar	

Sift the flour, baking powder, salt and sugar together into a bowl. Cut in shortening with a pastry blender and mix to a fine consistency. Add milk and knead into a soft dough. Transfer to a lightly floured board and roll ½ inch thick. Cut with a 2-inch cookie cutter into rounds. Place on a greased cookie sheet, leaving space for expansion between the biscuits. Bake for about 12 or 15 minutes in hot oven preheated to 425°F. Yield: 16 to 18.

NOTE: This is the baking powder biscuit recipe that Dad got from the boarding house mistress that I told you about on page

6. Biscuits made this way are wonderful . . . but frankly today's prepackaged biscuits are almost as good and not nearly so much work.

Green Lake Beefburger

2 lbs. ground beef
1 raw carrot, shredded
2 tbs. bread crumbs
½ tsp. monosodium gluta-
mate
6 drops Worcestershire
sauce
¼ tsp. salt
¼ tsp. freshly ground pepper
2 eggs

Put ground beef in a mixing bowl, add all other ingredients and mix until completely combined. Divide into four patties. Place on broiler pan and broil at 500°F. until rare, medium or well done, as desired. Serves 4.

N O T E : This recipe is wonderful, not only for its taste but also for its versatility. For example, it can be cooked over charcoal on a patio grill or over a campfire; it can be served on a toasted bun or in a sandwich with just about anything you want to go with it . . . raw or broiled onions, catsup or mustard, sliced tomato, lettuce, pickle relish, cucumber. Or it can be served on a plate with cooked vegetables as a main course. Instead of being broiled, it can be put into a casserole and baked for about 1 hour at 350°F. for a very tasty meat loaf.

Ham and Sweet Potato Patties

3 cups sweet potatoes,
mashed and seasoned to
taste
1 egg
3 cups baked or boiled
ham, ground
16 slices canned pineapple
16 slices bacon

121

Form mashed sweet potatoes into 8 patties of equal size. Break raw egg into ground ham and mix well. Form into 8 patties same size as others. Place a ham patty on a pineapple slice and a sweet potato patty on each ham patty. Top with remaining 8 slices of pineapple. Tie each stack together by crisscrossing 2 slices of bacon around each and fastening with wooden toothpicks. Place them in 2-inch-deep baking dish with about ¼ inch of space between stacks. Cover dish with aluminum foil and bake at 350°F. for 1 hour. Yield: 8 patties.

Beefsteak Pie

4 tbs. shortening	3 cups hot water
1½ lbs. beef, cut into bite-size pieces	4 tbs. all-purpose flour
	6 tbs. cold water
4 medium onions, sliced thin	1 tb. catsup
	Pastry crust (recipe follows)
2 tsps. salt	
¼ tsp. pepper	

Melt shortening in deep skillet until it sizzles. Add beef pieces and onion slices and turn until brown on all sides. Add salt, pepper and hot water. Cover and simmer 2 hours. Set meat aside in 2-quart casserole. Blend flour and cold water to a smooth paste in a mixing bowl, then stir into gravy remaining in skillet. Boil 1 minute, stirring constantly. Stir in catsup, pour over meat in casserole and set aside to cool while making pastry crust.

BEEFSTEAK PIE PASTRY CRUST

1 cup all-purpose flour	⅓ cup shortening
½ tsp. salt	3 tbs. cold water

Sift flour and salt together. Cut in shortening with pastry blender or knife until mixture forms into beads slightly larger than buckshot. Sprinkle with water and toss lightly with fork. Press dough firmly into a ball. Roll out to fit top of casserole dish. Cover meat with crust. Poke or cut air vents in crust with fork tines or knife tip. Bake 10 minutes at 450°F., reduce oven heat to 350° and bake 35 minutes longer. Serves 4.

Mr. Parris's Stuffed Pancakes

PART ONE: THE PANCAKES

¾ cup flour	Dash of nutmeg
2 eggs	1 tsp. olive oil
2 cups milk	Butter as needed
¼ tsp. salt	

Thoroughly mix all ingredients, except butter, in bowl. Heat griddle very hot, lightly grease with butter and add batter, 2 tbs. per pancake, and brown slightly on each side. Set aside and repeat until batter is used up.

PART TWO: THE FILLING

2 tbs. butter	2 tbs. crumbs made by
1 medium onion, chopped fine	crushing zwieback with rolling pin
1 lb. ground beef	2 hard-boiled eggs,
½ cup tomato puree	chopped fine
¼ cup sherry wine	½ cup grated Greek
1 tb. lemon juice	Kafaloteri cheese (if
Salt and pepper to taste	unavailable, use Italian
Dash of nutmeg	Parmesan)
½ tsp. parsley flakes	

Melt butter in skillet. Add onion and brown; add meat and stir constantly until brown. Stir in puree, wine, lemon juice, salt, pepper, nutmeg and parsley and cook 20 minutes. Allow to cool slightly. Stir in crumbs, eggs and cheese. Set aside and prepare . . .

123

PART THREE: TOMATO-SAUCE TOPPING

1 cup tomato puree ¼ cup sherry wine
2 cups beef stock or bouil- Salt to taste
lon Dash of nutmeg
½ tb. lemon juice ⅛ tsp. sugar

Combine all ingredients in saucepan and, stirring constantly, cook over low heat until thick. Set aside.

PART FOUR: PUTTING THEM ALL TOGETHER

All of the products of Parts Kafaloteri or Parmesan
One, Two and Three cheese (a goodly supply,
¼ lb. melted butter grated)

Spread 1 tb. of meat filling loosely on each pancake. Roll and fasten with wooden toothpicks, inserting them parallel to rolled-up cakes, not perpendicular. Place the meat-filled pancake fingers on a lightly greased baking sheet, brush with melted butter, sprinkle amply with cheese and bake in 350°F. oven until brown. Meanwhile keep tomato sauce hot on top of stove. When fingers are done, place them on platter, pour sauce over them, and serve. Serves 4 to 6.

Rotisserie Roasted Leg of Veal

½ pint white wine 1 5- to 7-lb. leg of veal (if
1 clove garlic too long or too heavy for
Salt and pepper to taste your rotisserie, have
 butcher cut off chops)
 2 tbs. Dijon mustard

Combine wine, garlic, salt and pepper, and marinate veal in the mixture—in the refrigerator—for a minimum of 5 hours, turning meat two or three times. Run rotisserie skewer through center of leg, along the bone, making both sides as nearly the same weight as possible. Insert meat thermometer into thickest part of meat, setting it in so that it will clear all sides of rotisserie as it turns, and so that it touches neither skewer nor bone. Pour wine marinade into dripping pan and add 1 cup of water—less if this amount will run over. (Use this liquid for making gravy to go with roast.) Spread mustard over entire leg and roast at 350°F. for 30 minutes; brush with marinade from dripping pan and roast at 450°F. for 30 minutes. Baste again, turn down to 350°F. heat for 1 hour or until meat thermometer registers 170°F. Serves 6 to 8.

Toots Shor's Hungarian Goulash

6 lbs. boneless shin beef, cut in cubes (about 1")
5 lbs. chopped onions (or less, if you desire)
1½ cups flour
4 tbs. paprika
Salt and pepper to taste
1 medium green pepper, finely chopped (optional)
1 tsp. caraway seeds (optional)
6 cups beef consommé

Spread beef cubes over bottom of very lightly greased roasting pan. Put in oven preheated to 450°F., cook until beef has started to brown and then add chopped onion. When meat is nicely browned, sprinkle flour and paprika over it. Continue cooking 2 or 3 minutes longer in the oven. Then transfer beef and onions to Dutch oven or heavy pot. Add salt and pepper. If a sharp taste is desired, add finely chopped green pepper and caraway seed. Add consommé. If not enough to cover contents of pot, add water. Cook on top of the stove for 2 to 2½ hours, simmering slowly. Serve about 10.

The Lambs' Irish Lamb Stew

2 lbs. cubed lamb meat from forequarter of lamb

2 carrots, scraped and cut in 1-inch pieces

2 stalks celery, cut in 1-inch pieces

1 medium onion, cut in 1-inch cubes

1 small bay leaf

1 small clove garlic, chopped fine

Salt and pepper to taste

Put cubed lamb in water to cover. Bring to a boil and cook for 20 minutes. Remove meat from water and wash under cold water. Put in a clean pot (a large, heavy one), add 3 quarts hot water and return to stove. Add carrots, celery, onion, bay leaf and garlic. Bring to a boil, turn down to simmer and cook uncovered for 1 hour. Season with salt and pepper. Serves 4 to 6.

Saito's Beef Sukiyaki

SAUCE:

1 cup beef soup stock (dashi) or beef consommé

½ cup Japanese-type soy sauce (shoyu)

½ cup Japanese cooking wine (mirin) *

1 heaping tsp. sugar

½ tsp. monosodium glutamate

OTHER SUKIYAKI INGREDIENTS:

3 ozs. beef suet

1 Bermuda onion, cut into ¼-inch-thick slices

12 scallions, cut in 2-inch lengths

2 cups canned shirataki (vermicelli)

4 large mushrooms, sliced

1 small can bamboo shoots, cut into thin strips

1 fresh bean curd (tofu), cut in 1-inch cubes

1½ lbs. tenderloin of beef, sliced very thin

1 small bunch watercress

Cooked rice for 4

1 raw egg, beaten (optional)

* If Japanese cooking wine is not available, dry sherry may be substituted.

To make sauce, mix together soup stock, soy sauce, wine, sugar and monosodium glutamate and stir. Pour into small pitcher and set aside.

Carry other Sukiyaki ingredients to living room or dining room on large tray and prepare Sukiyaki in front of guests, using an electric skillet. Guests may dip into skillet (with chopsticks) and extract appealing morsels as you cook.

Cut suet into small pieces and place in hot (400°F.) electric skillet. When suet is melted, add enough of the sauce to cover bottom of skillet. Add onion and scallions and cook 1 to 2 minutes. Add remaining sauce, vermicelli, mushrooms, bamboo shoots and bean curd and cook for 3 to 4 minutes. Add beef and cook 3 to 4 minutes longer or until meat just loses its red color. Add watercress and serve within a minute or two over bowls of hot rice. Divide juice from skillet over bowls of Sukiyaki. (Japanese like to dip bits of hot Sukiyaki into beaten raw egg just before eating them.) Serves 4.

N O T E : Although Sukiyaki is good made with substitute ingredients, it's at its best with Japanese or Japanese type soy sauce and wine.

Hamburger "21"

2 lbs. chopped top round steak	½ cup cold water
2 stalks chopped, cooked celery	1 tsp. Worcestershire sauce
2 whole eggs, lightly beaten	Salt and pepper to taste
	Butter as required for sautéing

Combine all ingredients except butter. Shape into 4 hamburger patties and sauté in butter. Serve with fresh string beans. Serves 4.

127

Carmen Prelee's Baked Meat Balls

1 lb. ground chuck
4 slices stale bread
(soaked in water and
squeezed out)
1 clove garlic, crushed
1 tsp. fresh parsley

½ tsp. sweet basil, dry
¼ cup grated Parmesan
cheese
1 egg
1 tsp. salt
1 tsp. black pepper

Mix first 2 ingredients together. Mix remaining ingredients together then stir into meat mixture. Shape into balls slightly larger than walnuts. Place in jelly roll or similar-type pan and bake in 350°F. oven for 30 minutes. While meat balls are baking, prepare Spaghetti Sauce (recipe follows).

Carmen Prelee's Spaghetti Sauce

2 tbs. salad oil
2 cloves garlic, chopped
2 12-oz. cans tomato paste
4½ cups water
½ cup grated Parmesan
cheese
1 bay leaf
2 tsps. chopped parsley
2 tsps. sweet basil

Salt and pepper to taste
1 lb. sausage (either sweet
or hot, or some of each,
to taste), cut up
1 beef shank that has been
cooked in oiled skillet
for about ½ hour until
lightly browned

Heat salad oil in a large roasting pan. Add garlic and sauté until light golden brown. Add tomato paste, water, grated cheese, bay leaf (remove bay leaf before serving), parsley, basil, salt and pepper, meatballs (see preceding recipe), sausage and beef shank. Bake in 350°F. oven for 3 to 4 hours until all ingredients are thoroughly blended. Additional water should be added if consistency becomes too thick. Serves 8 to 10.

N O T E : This sauce develops a fine, rich flavor and, since it needs no stirring, the meat balls retain their shape and the sauce never scorches as top-of-the-stove sauces sometimes do.

Mary Ameche's Veal Ragout

4 tbs. butter
2½ lbs. very lean veal, cut into 3-inch squares about ¾ inch thick
1½ cups thinly sliced onions
3 tbs. flour
2 cups water

1 4-oz. can mushrooms
1 6-oz. can tomato paste
⅛ tsp. marjoram
⅛ tsp. allspice
1½ tsps. salt
2 tsps. sugar
1 9-oz. pkg. frozen French-style string beans

Melt butter in large skillet over medium heat. When it starts to sizzle, add veal and onions, reduce heat to low, and cook gently until veal browns lightly on both sides. Sprinkle veal with flour. Combine water, drained mushrooms, tomato paste and slowly add to skillet, stirring to blend well. Then add marjoram, allspice, salt and sugar. Cover and cook, still on low heat, for about 45 minutes. Add string beans and cook another 15 minutes or until veal is tender. Serve with rice. Serves 8.

Mary Ameche's Tamale Pie

1 cup yellow cornmeal
1 cup cold water
3 cups boiling water
2 lbs. hamburger meat
¼ tsp. garlic powder
1 medium green pepper, chopped

1 medium onion, chopped
2 tbs. chili powder
1 6-oz. can tomato paste
1 7½-oz. can ripe olives, sliced, liquid reserved
Salt and cayenne pepper to taste

Stir cornmeal into cold water and soak for 20 minutes. Slowly add mixture to boiling water, stirring constantly until smooth. Cook until meal is the consistency of mashed potatoes. Brown hamburger meat in a large, heavy skillet, stirring often. As it cooks, add garlic powder, chopped green pepper, chopped onion, chili powder, tomato paste, sliced olives, reserved liquid and salt and cayenne pepper to taste. Continue cooking meat until liquid cooks down and it is moist but not runny. Pour cornmeal mixture into a greased casserole, top with meat mixture and bake ½ hour in preheated 300°F. oven. Serves 6.

NOTE: This pie tastes best when prepared the day before it is to be eaten, then reheated at serving time.

POULTRY

Roast Chicken with Cherries

1 5- or 6-lb. roasting
  chicken, including liver
Peanut oil, as needed
1 1-lb. 14-oz. can dark,
  sweet, pitted Bing cherries

2 tbs. cornstarch
½ cup chopped onion
1 clove garlic, crushed
2 tbs. red wine

Broil chicken liver, chop fine and set aside. Brush chicken with peanut oil, place on rack in roasting pan and roast in preheated 325°F. oven about 25–30 minutes per pound. Baste occasionally with drippings or with more oil if necessary. Separate cherries from syrup and add just enough syrup to the cornstarch to blend until smooth. Return mixture to remaining syrup and set aside. Heat 2 tbs. oil in a large skillet. Add onion and garlic and sauté on medium heat for 5 minutes. Remove skillet from heat, add chopped liver, stir in cornstarch-and-syrup mixture and wine and heat until thickened. Stir in cherries and bring to a boil. Place chicken on platter, pour skillet contents over it and serve. Serves 6 to 8.

Fried Walnut Chicken

(Jow Hop Tao Ghi)

1 tsp. salt
Dash of pepper
1 tb. brandy or gin
1 small egg
2 tbs. finely cut green
onion (scallion)
1 tsp. grated ginger root or
¾ tsp. ginger powder
4 tbs. flour

2 tbs. cornstarch
3 large chicken breasts,
boned and cut into
pieces about 1½ inches
long, 1 inch wide and
½ inch thick
¾ cup shelled walnuts
1 quart oil

Combine all but chicken, walnuts and oil and mix well to batter consistency. Place chicken pieces in the mixture, stir to cover evenly and let stand 15 minutes. Cover walnuts with boiling water, soak for 2 minutes, then skin nut meats and place on absorbent paper to dry. Pour oil into deep heavy skillet, wok or Dutch oven and, using a deep-fat thermometer, heat to 350°F. Add skinned walnuts and stir gently until lightly browned, about 1 or 2 minutes. Set browned nuts aside on absorbent paper and increase temperature of oil to 375°F. Stir chicken once or twice more in batter to ensure total coating and drop, piece by piece, into hot oil. Fry until golden brown, about 8 to 10 minutes. Arrange chicken on platter, top with walnuts, garnish with green leaf vegetable such as parsley or shredded lettuce or even green onion curls and serve with soy sauce and Chinese mustard as dips. Serves 6.

Braised Chicken, Purple Plums

¼ cup oil
1 3- to 4-lb. fryer, cut into
small serving pieces
1 1-lb. 14-oz. can whole
purple plums

½ cup soy sauce
⅓ cup sliced green onion
(scallions)
1 clove garlic, crushed
1 tb. cornstarch

Heat oil in large skillet, dip chicken pieces in soy sauce and sauté until brown. Drain plums while chicken is cooking, saving 1 cup of syrup. Chop enough of the plums to make ½ cup. Cut remaining plums in half, discard pits, and set aside. Combine soy sauce, sliced scallions, chopped plums, ½ cup syrup and garlic. Add the mixture to the browned chicken in the skillet and cook over low heat about 45 minutes to 1 hour, or until done. Remove chicken to warm serving platter while preparing sauce. Serves 4 to 6.

SAUCE: Combine cornstarch with remaining ½ cup plum syrup, stirring until smooth. Add this to drippings in skillet along with plum halves. Cook over low heat, stirring constantly until thick, about 2 minutes. Pour over chicken.

Duck in Orange-and-Wine Sauce

1 4-lb. duck	1 tsp. salt
1 cup orange juice	1 seedless orange, sliced
½ cup port wine	but unskinned

Rinse duck inside and out with cold tap water. Pat dry with paper towels, truss and place on rack in roasting pan. Combine orange juice, wine and salt while oven is preheating to 350°F. Place pan in oven and immediately pour juice-and-wine mixture over duck. Roast 2 hours and 20 minutes, basting at 10-minute intervals with sauce from bottom of pan. Ten minutes before duck is done, arrange orange slices around it on the rack, but make sure they are not in the sauce. When done, place duck on serving platter and garnish with the orange slices. Serves 4.

Chicken à la Newburg

4 tbs. butter
2 cups leftover chicken, boned and cut in large pieces
¼ tsp. salt
⅛ tsp. pepper
Dash cayenne
4 tbs. sherry wine

½ cup sliced mushrooms
1 cup medium cream
3 egg yolks
4 slices buttered toast or patty shells
Grated Parmesan cheese (optional)
Paprika (optional)

Melt butter in chafing dish or double boiler. Add chicken. Sprinkle with salt, pepper and cayenne, add 2 tbs. sherry and all of mushroom slices, stir and cook 2 minutes. Beat egg yolks with cream and remaining sherry, stir into chicken mixture and cook 3 minutes more. Stir well and spoon onto toast slices or into patty shells. Sprinkle lightly with Parmesan cheese and/or paprika, if desired. Serves 4.

VARIATIONS: Lobster, crab meat, shrimp, turkey or duck may be substituted for chicken. Or, for that matter, any similar type of leftover.

Chicken Cakes

(Here's a recipe that my Dad picked up somewhere in the Midwest —just where I do not know. The name is strictly American, but the ingredients add a touch that smacks of the Balkans. I'll never know if the recipe came originally from there. But this I learned long ago: it tastes grand.)

4 uncooked chicken breasts
3 tbs. bread crumbs
½ pint heavy cream
¼ tsp. nutmeg
1 tsp. freshly ground black pepper

1 tsp. salt
3 egg whites
Flour
⅛ lb. butter

Bone the chicken breasts. Coarsely grind chicken and combine with bread crumbs, cream, nutmeg, pepper and salt in a bowl and mix well. Form into cakes about ½ inch thick and dust lightly with flour. Add butter to skillet and, when it starts to sizzle, sauté each cake at medium heat until nicely golden brown on each side. Serves 4.

Tori Gohan

(Chicken with Rice Japanese Style)

1 lb. uncooked chicken, cut into small pieces	2 tbs. soy sauce
½ cup soy sauce	1 tsp. monosodium gluta-mate
3 cups uncooked rice	½ cup diced mushrooms
4 cups water	1 cup cooked peas

Marinate chicken in the ½ cup soy sauce for 1 hour. Soak rice in 4 cups of water for 1 hour before putting on stove and bringing to a boil. Add the 2 tbs. soy sauce, monosodium glutamate and mushrooms to the rice and mix thoroughly. Place chicken pieces on top of the rice, cover, lower the heat and let steam until chicken is tender (about 20–30 minutes). Then remove chicken, transfer rice to platter, place chicken on rice and garnish with hot cooked peas. Serves 4.

Chicken Teriyaki

1 2- to 3-lb. frying chicken	½ tsp. powdered ginger
½ cup soy sauce	2 tsps. rye whiskey or dry sherry
6 tbs. sugar	
1 slice raw ginger or	

Cut the chicken into serving-size pieces. Combine all other ingredients and marinate the chicken in the mixture for several hours.

Pat chicken dry with lint-free towel and broil for 45 minutes, either over charcoal or in preheated broiler, basting frequently with the marinade. Serves 4.

N O T E : For a glazed coat that's mighty pleasing to the eye, remove the skin of the chicken before marinating.

Chicken Chili Casserole

¼ cup flour
1 tsp. salt
¼ tsp. pepper
1 tsp. chili powder, or to taste
1 tsp. dry thyme

1 4-lb. chicken, cut into pieces
2 tbs. shortening
½ cup milk
Minced parsley

Combine flour, salt, pepper, chili powder and thyme. Spread on wax paper and roll chicken pieces in mixture until well coated. Save excess mixture for gravy. Melt shortening in deep frying pan until it sizzles. Add chicken and turn until brown on all sides. Transfer chicken to casserole and add hot water until ¾ covered. Cover (use aluminum foil if casserole dish has no lid) and bake at 325°F. for 3 hours or until tender. Transfer chicken to heated platter and set aside. Skim fat from liquid left in casserole and discard. Add hot water to liquid to make 1 cup. Mix 2 tbs. leftover flour mixture with 3 tbs. cold water and stir until smooth and thick. Stir in milk. Pour gravy over chicken and garnish with minced parsley. Serves 6.

Baked Chicken, Greek Style

1 5-lb. roasting chicken
Juice of ½ lemon
Salt and pepper to taste
2 cups hot water

2 tbs. olive oil
2 tbs. melted butter
¼ tsp. oregano or marjoram

Wash chicken inside and out and dry with lint-free towel. Mix lemon juice, salt and pepper and rub into chicken both inside and out. Let stand for 1 hour. Pour hot water, olive oil and butter into baking pan, place chicken on its back in rack and put in pan. Sprinkle with oregano or marjoram, cover, and bake for 1½ hours at 375°F. Baste frequently. Serves 4.

Meat, Nut and Raisin Dressing

(Try this one of two ways and love both of them: as a meal in itself or as a stuffing for a bird)

¼ lb. butter	3 whole cloves
1 medium-to-large onion, chopped	3 tbs. chopped parsley
	1 cinnamon stick
1 clove garlic, chopped	2 cups cooked rice
½ lb. ground beef	½ cup slivered almonds
½ lb. ground pork	½ cup cooked chestnuts, chopped
Salt and pepper to taste	
2 tbs. tomato paste diluted with ½ tb. water	½ cup white raisins

Melt butter in large pan. Add onion and garlic and sauté until translucent. Add beef, pork, salt and pepper and stir constantly over medium heat until pink color is gone, about 10–15 minutes. Stir in diluted tomato paste. Add cloves, parsley and cinnamon, cover and cook on low heat 45 to 60 minutes or until meat is very nearly done. Then stir in rice, cook 10 minutes more, stir in almonds, chestnuts and raisins and cook another 5 minutes. Serve hot as a main dish. Serves 4 to 6. Allow to cool before using to stuff a 4- to 5-lb. bird.

Toots Shor's Potted Chicken

6 tbs. cooking oil	8 ounces white wine
3 tbs. butter	3 tbs. cornstarch or as
3 2½-lb. chickens	needed (use about 2 to
Salt and pepper	3 tsps. per cup of liquid
1 to 1½ quarts consommé	to thicken gravy)
4 lbs. mushrooms, cleaned	
and quartered	

Put 2 tbs. cooking oil and 1 tb. butter in each of 2 or 3 large, heavy skillets and heat until butter blends into oil. Cut up chicken, season it to taste, and brown on both sides. Transfer chicken to large, heavy pot and cover with consommé. Add quartered mushrooms and simmer for ½ hour, or until tender. After chicken is cooked, add white wine. Thicken gravy with cornstarch. Serves 8.

Faisan à la Choucroute "21"

PART ONE

1 1½-lb. young pheasant	1 pinch salt
1 slice lard	1 tb. corn oil
1 pinch rosemary	3 bay leaves

Clean and truss pheasant. Place slice of lard across breast and put pheasant in a roasting pan. Sprinkle with rosemary and salt, brush with corn oil; put bay leaves on breast and roast for about 25 minutes in oven preheated to 400°F. Baste 3 or 4 times. When golden brown on one side turn over and continue cooking until other side is also a rich golden color. Remove from pan and set aside. Leave drippings in roasting pan, but take out of oven so they won't get too dark. Serves 1 or 2.

PART TWO: SAUCE

½ cup flour
Drippings (from above)
Salt and pepper to taste

1 cup white wine (or
sherry)
1 cup chicken broth
(or thin brown gravy)

Sprinkle flour into the drippings. Stir in salt and pepper and cook on top of stove, stirring constantly. (If you don't want to use your oven pan on stove top, pour just enough chicken broth into it to help loosen bits of scrapings and then transfer with all grease to a heavy skillet.) Add wine and simmer for a few minutes, continuing to stir. Heat 1 cup chicken broth to boiling and add all at once to gravy, stirring constantly until it thickens. Then continue cooking at a lowered heat for 15 minutes. Stir occasionally. Strain and set aside. Makes sauce for 2 to 4 servings.

PART THREE: SAUERKRAUT

For each 1½-lb. pheasant
to be cooked, prepare:
1 tsp. butter

1 small onion, sliced
1 cup of canned sauerkraut
¼ tsp. caraway seeds

Melt butter in heavy skillet. When very hot but not burning, add onion and sauté until light golden color. Stir in other ingredients. Heat for 15 minutes, stirring occasionally. Drain and then set aside.

TO SERVE, FOR EACH PERSON, YOU WILL NEED:

1 slice Genoa salami
1 to 2 small boiled potatoes

½ cup cooked baby car-
rots, sliced

Place drained sauerkraut in center of ovenware serving dish. Surround with pheasants. Across each breast place one slice of salami. Garnish with potatoes and carrots. Pour gravy over entire dish and place in 350°F. oven until piping hot. Serve at once.

N O T E : If pheasant is to be halved and served to two people, it may be easier and look nicer if you do the cutting before gravy is poured over dish and it is put in oven to heat.

Saito's Mizutaki

1 3-lb. chicken cut into 1½-inch cubes, bones left in
Salt to taste
6 scallions, cut in 1-inch lengths

1 medium-size onion, peeled and sliced thin
1 bunch watercress, trimmed
Hot cooked rice for 4

SAUCE:

1 cup lemon juice
1 cup soy sauce
1 tsp. monosodium glutamate

Japanese wine (sake) to taste

Place pieces of chicken in a heavy saucepan and cover with water. Add salt to taste and simmer gently for 45 minutes after the boiling point is reached. Bring to the table in an electric skillet or in the utensil in which it was cooked and place over a charcoal or alcohol burner so that the liquid barely boils. Combine sauce ingredients, mix well and set aside.

When guests are seated, add vegetables to the simmering broth, a few at a time. To serve, spoon a few portions of the meat and barely cooked vegetables into small serving bowls. Using chopsticks or forks, guests dip bite-size bits of chicken into the sauce. Serve hot rice in separate bowls. Serves 4.

The Lambs' Chicken in the Pot

4 2½-lb. broiling chickens
3 large carrots, scraped
3 medium onions
8 celery stalks
Salt and pepper to taste
Monosodium glutamate to taste

4 ozs. medium noodles (cook according to package instructions, but be sure water is boiling before adding noodles)
Matzo balls (see recipe below)

Wash chickens inside and out and put in a heavy pot with carrots, onions and celery. Cover with cold water, add salt and pepper, bring to a boil and cook until chicken is tender (about 25 minutes). Add monosodium glutamate to taste. Remove chicken and vegetables and cool. Remove skin and bones from chicken. Cut vegetables into julienne strips. Strain broth and set aside. Meanwhile, make matzo balls and cook noodles.

Place cooked noodles in deep casserole. Put matzo balls on top and cover with deboned chicken and julienne vegetable strips. Pour chicken broth over it all, filling casserole as full as you can without danger of the contents boiling over. Cover pot and simmer for 20 to 30 minutes. Serve piping hot. Serves 8.

MATZO BALLS

1 cup cold water	1 cup chicken fat
5 eggs	6 ozs. matzo meal

Pour cold water into mixing bowl. Break eggs into water, add chicken fat and beat ingredients together. Pour matzo meal into the mixture. Beat well and empty into small pan. Refrigerate for 1 hour. Remove from refrigerator and form into small balls. Put 1 quart water in large pot and bring to boil. Carefully add matzo balls, one by one. Turn down to a low boil and cook 30 minutes.

Turkey with Chestnut Stuffing

(*Dinde farcie aux marrons à notre manière*)

(A good stuffing will make a turkey even more enjoyable. Here is a recipe for one that is outstanding, in my opinion.)

141

1 young hen turkey, 10 to
  12 lbs.
DRESSING:
  Giblets
  Salt and pepper
  Pinch thyme
  Bay leaf
  Spiced salt

1½ cups bacon fat,
  strained
2 shallots, chopped
1½ lbs. lean pork
2 tbs. brandy
2 lbs. chestnuts
1 stalk celery, chopped
Stock
Bacon slices

Wash neck and giblets. Prepare giblets as follows: Cut liver into six pieces, season with salt, pepper, thyme and add bay leaf; set aside on a plate. Cut gizzard in half, remove tough inner membrane and discard. Chop gizzard and heart finely. Dice lean pork and sprinkle with spiced salt. Set these giblets aside separately.

Melt 2 tbs. bacon fat in a frying pan and when it is hot, toss in liver; brown quickly on the outside, keeping inside pink. Remove liver with a perforated spoon, set aside to cool and then chop very fine. Add tablespoon bacon fat to pan and lightly fry the shallots. Add diced pork, chopped gizzard, and heart and stir continuously over a high flame until about half-cooked. Remove from heat and immediately pour in the brandy. Light it, and cover pan immediately with a tight-fitting lid. Allow to cool, then add to liver together with bacon fat (about a cupful). Stir and blend well.

Slit chestnuts on the domed side and put in a baking tin with a little water; roast in a hot oven for 8 minutes. Peel chestnuts while still hot and put in a pan with the chopped celery; add enough stock to cover and simmer gently. Do not overcook. Stop while chestnuts are still firm. Drain, add to stuffing mixture and blend carefully so as to keep chestnuts whole. Season turkey inside with pepper and salt, then stuff and truss it. Cover breast with bacon slices, holding them in place with toothpicks. Place bird on its side in a roasting pan together with the neck. Brush with remaining bacon fat and sprinkle with salt. Cover and roast in a medium over (375°F.); allow about 20 minutes per pound.

Turn the bird often and toward the end of cooking period, uncover, remove bacon and allow the breast to brown evenly. To test if it is done, pierce thigh; when clear juice runs out with no tinge of pink, the bird is done. Remove trussing, skim off and discard surplus fat from pan juices; serve juice with turkey. Serves 8 to 10.

SEAFOOD

Most of us do not eat nearly enough fish, although its health-giving qualities are beyond dispute. Doctors and nutritionists agree that everyone, particularly children, should eat fish at least four times a week.

The trouble is that most people think they don't like fish . . . because they rarely get to eat fish that is properly cooked. So here are some easy pointers to remember, compiled by my co-author, Dan Morris, who also co-authored a seafood cookbook, *The Savor of the Sea:*

1. The fresher the fish, the better the taste.

2. In frying with oil, make sure the oil is clean.

3. Never allow any shortening, whether it be oil, butter, lard or margarine, to get so hot as to start smoking.

4. Most fish recipes are interchangeable. The best fish to use, no matter what fish a recipe may call for, is the fish that's in season in waters closest to your home.

5. Test fish for doneness with a fork, not with a clock. Poke the fattest part gently with the tines, and when the flesh flakes easily immediately remove the fish from the heat.

6. Times given in fish recipes are only a general guide because the sizes and shapes of fish vary. Always start testing with a fork at half the given time.

7. Introduce children to fish with accepted, everyday foods such as tuna-fish sandwiches. Then, as their taste for fish develops, gradually add other seafood dishes to their diets.

Shrimp Creole with Saffron Rice

¼ cup bacon drippings
2 medium onions, finely chopped
1 clove garlic, finely chopped
2 large green peppers, seeded and coarsely chopped
1 cup chopped celery
1 10-oz. can tomatoes
1 6-oz. can tomato paste

¼ cup chopped parsley
2 tsps. salt
¼ tsp. pepper
1 tsp. paprika
2 lbs. large shrimp, shelled and deveined
1 10-oz. package frozen cut okra, thawed and drained
1 tsp. gumbo filé powder

Melt bacon drippings in heavy pot and, when it starts to sizzle but does not smoke, add onions, garlic, peppers and celery and sauté until tender, stirring occasionally. Add tomatoes, tomato paste and parsley and simmer until thick, about 30 to 45 minutes, stirring occasionally. Add salt, pepper and paprika. Stir, add shrimp, and 2 minutes later add okra. Cover and cook 5 minutes more. Finally stir in gumbo filé powder to thicken slightly and immediately spoon onto bed of saffron rice (recipe follows) or in center of saffron rice ring. Serves 6.

Saffron Rice

4 cups chicken soup stock
3 tbs. butter
¼ tsp. crumbled saffron

Salt to taste
2 cups long grain rice, uncooked

Bring stock to a boil. Add butter, saffron, salt and rice. Cover pot with tight-fitting lid, turn heat to low and cook 20 to 25 minutes or until rice is tender and liquid is absorbed.

For a saffron rice ring, spoon rice lightly into a 6-cup buttered ring mold and let stand 1 minute. Unmold on heated platter, fill center with shrimp creole or whatever else suits your mood, and serve. Serves 6.

The Waldorf-Astoria's Bull and Bear Room Curried Shrimp

¼ lb. butter
1 clove garlic, crushed
1 large onion, finely chopped
3 stalks celery, chopped
1 green pepper, seeded and chopped
2 apples, cored, peeled and quartered
1 carrot, sliced
2 tomatoes, halved and sliced
1 tb. chopped parsley
1 bay leaf
Pinch thyme
Pinch marjoram
Pinch dried mint
2 whole cloves
¼ tsp. basil
2 tbs. flour
2 tbs. curry powder
½ tsp. salt
½ tsp. freshly ground pepper
¼ tsp. cayenne pepper
¼ tsp. nutmeg
2 cups consommé
1 cup dry white wine
2 lbs. fresh boiled shrimps, shelled and cleaned
3 cups boiled rice
Parsley for garnish
Chutney

Melt butter in a large saucepan. Add garlic, onion, celery, green pepper, 2 apples, carrot, tomatoes, chopped parsley, bay leaf, thyme, marjoram, dried mint, cloves and basil. Cook over low heat. When the vegetables are soft, sprinkle in flour mixed with curry powder, salt, pepper, cayenne pepper and nutmeg. Cook for about 5 minutes. Then slowly add 2 cups of consommé. When the mixture begins to thicken add wine. Cook over low heat for about ½ hour.

Now you can do one of two things. If you like a thin curry sauce, you can strain the above mixture into another saucepan, add shrimps and simmer about 10 minutes. On a platter make a ring of the boiled rice and pour the shrimp curry into the center of the ring. Sprinkle with finely chopped parsley and serve with chutney. The second choice is to add the shrimps to the sauce without straining it, let heat, and serve on individual plates over a mound of fluffy rice. Of course, chutney is also indicated with this method. Personally, I prefer the second choice. Serves 4.

Fried Shrimp, Japanese Style

(*Shrimp Tempura*)

3 cups flour	30 raw shrimp, shelled and
1¼ cups water	deveined
1 egg	Cooking oil, enough to fill
1 tsp. salt	deep fryer ¾ full
Pinch baking powder	

Combine 2 cups flour, water, egg, salt and baking powder and stir 3 minutes or until batter is velvety smooth. Wash shrimp and lightly pat dry. Pour remaining cup of flour into pie pan or onto wax paper and roll shrimp in it to dust on all sides. Dip shrimp in batter. Heat oil in deep fryer to 375°F. (use a deep-fat thermometer). Place shrimp in wire basket, lower into fat and deep-fry 2 minutes or until golden brown. Serve with rice, soy sauce and, for those who like it, horseradish. Serves 6.

Basic Seafood Cocktail Sauce

¼ tsp. Tabasco sauce	1 tb. horseradish, prefer-
1 cup catsup or chili sauce	ably red
2 tbs. lemon juice	1 tsp. grated onion

Combine tabasco with catsup or chili sauce. Mix well. Stir in the remaining ingredients until nicely blended. This should make enough for 4 average servings.

NOTE: This basic recipe can be varied in any way that your taste dictates to make it hotter, milder or whatever. Quantities can be changed proportionately to increase or decrease number of servings. The finished product makes an excellent dip or pour-over for shrimp, clams, oysters, crab meat or just about any cold-fish appetizer.

Salmon Steaks Baked in Tomato Sauce

4 salmon steaks, about
¾-inch thick
2 medium onions, sliced

½ stick butter or margarine
2 8-oz. cans tomato sauce

Lightly grease shallow baking pan and then place salmon steaks side by side in pan. Top with onion slices, dot butter or margarine over the onion and pour tomato sauce over all. Bake at 350°F. (moderate oven) 25 to 35 minutes or until fish flakes easily when tested with a fork. Serves 4.

N O T E : Any fish in season may be substituted for salmon, but they then should be baked about 20 to 25 minutes.

Smoked Fish, Sour Cream and Cheese Omelet

6 eggs
2 tbs. cold water
Pinch of pepper
Worcestershire sauce to
taste

½ cup flaked smoked fish
2 tbs. butter or margarine
½ cup sour cream
¼ cup grated cheese

Combine eggs, water, pepper and Worcestershire sauce in mixing bowl and beat lightly with fork. When nicely blended, stir in flaked fish. Melt butter or margarine in frying pan. When it starts to sizzle, pour in omelet mixture and cook at medium heat. As it begins to set, turn back edges gently with a knife to allow loose mixture to run down. When almost firm, turn off heat. Spread with sour cream, sprinkle with grated cheese and brown lightly in broiler, about 3 to 4 inches below flame, at 500°F. Serves 6.

Baked Clams Brittany

12 hardshell clams

2 tbs. butter

1 chopped shallot

1 tsp. minced parsley

2 tbs. white wine

Juice of 1 small lemon

⅛ tsp. salt or to taste

⅛ tsp. cayenne pepper or to taste

3 tbs. bread crumbs

Wash and scrub clam shells thoroughly in cold water. Remove meat from shells and poach 2 minutes in their own liquid, taking care that it does not boil. Set aside. Melt 1 tb. butter in small saucepan. Add shallot, parsley, wine, lemon juice, salt and pepper and simmer slowly until only about 1½ tbs. liquid remains. Brown bread crumbs lightly in remaining 1 tb. butter and combine with wine-and-lemon sauce. Replace each clam in a half shell, top each with bread crumb mixture, place on baking pan and bake in 500°F. oven until brown. Serves 2.

Water-Broiled Fish Fillets with Sour Cream

½ cup hot water

4 fish fillets*, ½ inch thick

Salt and pepper to taste

2 tbs. melted butter

1 cup sour cream

1 tomato, sliced thin

Parsley, either sprigs or chopped, for garnish

Pour hot water into shallow aluminum broiler pan that has either wire rack or perforated metal rack. Be sure water does not come above level of rack. Season fillets on both sides with salt and pepper, place on rack and brush top side with melted butter. Spread sour cream over fillets, slide pan into broiler so that cream-topped fillets are 3 to 4 inches below source of heat and broil at 500°F. for about 5 minutes or until fish flakes easily when tested with a fork. Place fillets on platter, surround with tomato slices, garnish with parsley and serve. Serves 4.

* Any fish in season is the fish to use in this little-known cooking method that broils fish on the top while steaming it on the bottom.

Tuna, Noodles and Nuts

2 tbs. oil
½ lb. mushrooms, sliced
½ cup sliced onion
½ cup finely sliced green pepper
3 cans (6½ or 7 ozs. each) chunk-style white meat tuna, drained
2 cans (11 ozs. each) cream of tomato soup, undiluted

½ cup milk
⅛ tsp. thyme
Salt to taste
½ cup sour cream
12 oz.-pkg. medium egg noodles
⅓ cup butter or margarine
½ cup coarsely chopped unsalted nuts of your choice*

Heat oil in skillet until it sizzles but does not smoke. Add mushrooms, onion and green pepper and sauté lightly. Then stir in tuna, soup, milk, thyme and salt and heat to serving temperature. Stir in sour cream and maintain at serving temperature while preparing noodles according to package directions. Use a clean skillet to melt butter. Then add chopped nuts, stir and toast lightly. Add nuts to noodles, toss gently, divide on six plates and top each with tuna sauce. Serves 6.

Shrimp Curry, Pakistan Style

1 lime
1 lb. raw shrimp, peeled and deveined
½ cup vegetable oil
1 onion, chopped
1 tsp. ginger
½ tsp. red pepper

½ tsp. finely chopped garlic
½ tsp. turmeric
1 tsp. salt
2 tbs. tomato paste
2 cups water

Squeeze lime juice over shrimp, stir once lightly and let stand while heating oil in skillet. When oil sizzles but does not smoke,

* We prefer hazelnuts at our house.

add shrimp and sauté lightly. Then remove from pan and set aside. Brown onion in the same oil in skillet, add ginger, pepper, garlic, turmeric and salt. Mix well. Add tomato paste and cook 5 minutes. Add water, bring to boil, reduce heat, add shrimp and cook about 10 minutes or until sauce thickens. Serve hot over rice. Serves 4.

Wine-and-Mushroom Marinated Fish Fillets

3 tbs. butter
1 tsp. oil
¼ lb. mushrooms, chopped
1 tb. chopped green pep-
per
½ cup chopped onion
6 tbs. white wine

2 lbs. fish fillets*
2 tbs. flour
Hot water
Salt and pepper to taste
Parsley, either sprigs or
chopped, for garnish
Lemon wedges

Combine butter and oil in skillet and heat until it sizzles but does not smoke. Add mushrooms, green pepper and onion and sauté lightly for 2 minutes. Pour wine into small mixing bowl and add sautéed vegetables, making transfer from skillet to bowl with slotted spoon so as to save liquid in frying pan. Then place fillets side by side in well-greased baking pan and pour wine mixture over them. Let stand 1 hour and then bake in 325°F. oven for no more than 20 minutes or until fish flakes easily when tested with a fork. Near the end of that time, reheat liquid in skillet and slowly blend in flour. When fillets are done, transfer them and the vegetables, again using slotted spoon for the latter, to a preheated platter. Combine liquid from baking pan with enough hot water to make 1 cup and add slowly to flour mixture in skillet. Stir constantly and cook slowly until sauce thickens. Cook about 5 minutes more, add salt and pepper, pour over fillets, garnish with parsley and lemon and serve. Serves 6.

* Any fish in season is fine, but flounder is best.

Fish Fillets Baked in Wine with Cheese and Mushrooms, Australian Style

1 lb. fish fillets*	1 tsp. cooking oil
¼ lb. grated cheese, mild	¼ lb. mushrooms, sliced
3 tbs. chopped shallots or white onions	4 tbs. white wine
	Chopped parsley for garnish
Salt and pepper to taste	
2 tsps. butter	1 lemon, cut into wedges

Lay the fillets in an evenly greased, shallow baking dish or pan and sprinkle first with the cheese, then with the shallots or onions and lastly with salt and pepper to taste. Set aside. Combine butter and cooking oil in a skillet and heat until it sizzles but does not smoke. Add sliced mushrooms and sauté lightly for two minutes, stirring constantly. Spread atop fish fillets. Pour wine over all and bake at 400°F. for no more than 15 minutes or until fish flakes easily when tested with a fork. Garnish with chopped parsley and serve with lemon wedges. Serves 4.

Tuna-and-Shrimp Soufflé

1 7-oz. (about) can of chunk-style white-meat tuna	3 eggs
	Dash of nutmeg
	Salt and pepper to taste
1 10-oz. can frozen shrimp soup	1 tb. (about) butter, margarine or oil

Drain tuna and break chunks into flakes with a fork and set aside. Defrost shrimp soup and empty can into top of double boiler. Separate eggs. Beat yolks well, add to soup, turn heat to low and stir constantly until mixture starts to simmer, taking care not to let it boil. Stir in tuna, nutmeg, salt and pepper and remove from heat.

* Any fish in season will do, but the lean ones such as flounder or whiting are best.

Beat egg whites until stiff but not dry, fold lightly into tuna-and-shrimp mixture and pour into soufflé pan or casserole dish that has been greased with shortening of your choice. Place baking pan of water in oven, set soufflé pan or casserole in the water, and bake in preheated oven at 350°F. about 45 minutes or until top is brown and center of soufflé is firm. Serves 4.

N O T E : It's better to buy chunk-style tuna and then flake it rather than buying flaked tuna. The chunk-style quality is better.

Bill Chan's Golden Shrimp

(Ingredients are divided into 2 parts for easier following)

NO. 1

¼ tsp. salt	1 tsp. light soy sauce
½ tsp. sugar	1 tsp. Worcestershire sauce
¼ tsp. monosodium gluta-mate	4 drops Tabasco sauce
	½ cup catsup

NO. 2

16 large shrimp	½ cup sliced onion
16 pieces of bacon, same size as shrimp	½ tb. dry sherry wine
2 tbs. vegetable oil	¾ cup chicken soup stock
2 eggs, slightly beaten	2 tbs. cornstarch dissolved in 1 tb. water
¼ tsp. salt	1 tb. crushed almonds
Dash pepper	2 tbs. chopped scallions

Combine all ingredients in No. 1, stir well, and set aside.

Shell shrimp but leave tail on. Slit underside to back but do not cut through. Flatten, devein, dip in cold water and pat dry with lint-free cloth towel. Press each shrimp down on a piece of bacon. (If desired all this may be done in advance and refrigerated.) Add 1 tb. oil to preheated skillet. Dip shrimp and bacon in beaten egg. When oil starts to sizzle place in pan, bacon side down. Fry until golden brown, then turn so bacon is up and fry 2 minutes more. Remove from heat and set aside.

Preheat saucepan, add remaining 1 tb. oil, salt, pepper and onion and stir until onions are translucent, taking care not to burn. Then, in order, add sherry, soup stock and No. 1 mixture, stir, and bring to a boil. Add cornstarch-and-water mixture and stir to consistency of heavy cream. Put through strainer into gravy bowl and sprinkle with almonds and scallions.

Place shrimp on platter garnished with lettuce leaves, bacon side down, and serve with sauce on side for dipping. Or, if you prefer, sauce may be poured over shrimp. Serves 4.

Chinese Pineapple Fish

2 tbs. peanut oil
4 green peppers, shredded
¼ cup canned bamboo shoots
¼ cup bean sprouts
¼ cup white vinegar
1 tb. brown sugar
1 tsp. powdered ginger
1 tsp. minced candied ginger
1 tb. soy sauce
1 lb. flounder fillets, ¼ to ½ inch thick and cut bite-size
1 cup pineapple cubes, drained
1 tb. cornstarch

Heat oil in chafing dish. Sauté peppers, bamboo shoots and bean sprouts. Add vinegar, sugar, ginger and soy sauce. Mix and cook until peppers are tender, stirring occasionally. Add fish. Stir and cook 8 minutes or until fish flakes easily when tested with a fork. Add pineapple. Stir and cook another 2 minutes. Push mixture to one side of pan, stir the cornstarch into the pan gravy, cook until thickened and swiftly combine with the pineapple-fish mixture. Serve at once on beds of crisp Chinese noodles or boiled rice. Serves 4.

Shrimp Curry in Papaya

⅓ cup butter
3 tbs. minced onion
1 stalk celery, finely
  chopped
1 tart apple, sliced
1 tb. curry powder
5 tbs. flour
½ tsp. dry mustard
1 clove garlic, crushed
1 bay leaf

3 whole cloves
1 tsp. salt
3 cups bouillon
1 lb. cooked shrimp, cut
  into about ¼- to ½-inch
  pieces
⅓ cup heavy cream
2 tbs. chutney
3 papayas

Melt butter in good-size saucepan. Add onion, celery and apple and sauté 10 minutes on medium heat, stirring often. Combine curry powder, flour, mustard, garlic, bay leaf, cloves and salt and stir into apple mixture. Slowly stir in bouillon until sauce thickens. Reduce heat and simmer 30 minutes. Remove bay leaf and cloves. Stir in shrimp, cream and chutney and cook another 5 minutes. Cut papayas in half, remove seeds and fill with curried shrimp mixture. Place in shallow baking pan and bake 10 to 15 minutes in 350°F. oven. Serves 6.

VARIATIONS: Oysters, clams, scallops or chicken for the shrimp; avocado for the papaya.

Salmon-Stuffed Baked Potatoes

4 large baking potatoes
2 7½-oz. (about) cans
  salmon
2 tbs. butter or margarine
⅓ cup milk

2 tsps. grated onion
Salt and pepper to taste
¼ cup grated cheddar
  cheese

Bake potatoes in 450°F.- to 500°F.-oven until pulp is tender (test with fork), about 45 to 60 minutes. Meantime transfer salmon, with liquid, to bowl and flake. Discard skin but mash in the bones (they're good for people, especially growing children). When potatoes are done, cut in half lengthwise and carefully scoop the meat into a bowl, taking care not to break the potato skin. Add butter or margarine, milk, onion, salt and pepper and mash well. Add the salmon and oils. Mix thoroughly. Pile the mixture high in each of the potato skins and sprinkle each with grated cheese. Turn oven to 450°F. and bake the stuffed halves until cheese is well melted. Serves 8.

The Hotel Roosevelt's Lobster à l'Américaine

10 live lobsters (1½ lbs. each)
3 cups oil
1 lb. carrots, coarsely chopped
1 lb. onions, coarsely chopped
1 lb. celery, coarsely chopped
Several sprigs parsley
¼ lb. shallots, finely chopped
4 cloves garlic, crushed to a pulp
2 bay leaves
1 tsp. thyme leaves
10 ozs. butter (2½ sticks)
2½ cups flour
1 cup cognac
2½ pints dry white wine
4 lbs. fresh tomatoes, coarsely chopped
1 quart tomato puree
1 gallon fish stock, broth or water
1 tb. salt
1 tb. whole black pepper, freshly ground
1 tb. parsley
1 tb. tarragon leaves

Detach claws from lobsters and remove tail from body. Break claws with the back of a knife and section tail across into 3 pieces; or, if you prefer, the tail may be left whole if the lobsters are small. Split the lobster heads, remove the green coral and the liver and reserve. Also remove the small bag found in the lobster head which usually contains sand.

Heat oil in a casserole and throw in the cut-up lobsters. Sauté until

157

the pieces get a nice red color. Add the carrots, onions and celery and a few sprigs of parsley. A few minutes later add the shallots, garlic, bay leaves and thyme. Meanwhile, melt butter in a saucepan and blend in the flour; cook 5 to 6 minutes over low heat while stirring and add to the lobster stew. When the vegetables are about half cooked, pour out cooking oil and flame mixture with cognac. When flame dies, add the white wine and cook to reduce by about half. Add the fresh tomatoes and tomato puree and cook just a few minutes. Then add the fish stock, a good broth or water. Add salt and pepper and bring to a boil. Cover and cook for about 18 to 20 minutes (cooking time depends on the size of the lobsters), remove lobster meat from shell, and keep hot. Put shells back in pot.

Strain the sauce, pressing on the lobster heads. Bring the sauce to another boil and blend in the livers and lobster coral crushed with some butter. Allow to cook a few minutes, but *do not allow to boil.* Add parsley and tarragon leaves and pour the sauce over the lobster pieces and serve very hot. Serves 10.

The Hotel Roosevelt's Baked Quiche Lorraine with Florida Crab Meat

2 tbs. shallots, finely chopped	2 level tbs. chopped chives
1 oz. butter	1 level tb. salt
½ cup dry white wine	1 tsp. white pepper, freshly ground
1½ lbs. Florida lump crab meat	¼ lb. shredded Swiss cheese
Juice of 2 lemons	1 prebaked 10″ pie shell, 1½″ deep
9 whole eggs	
1 quart light cream	

Sauté shallots in butter. Add wine. Cook till reduced to half its volume. Add crab meat, sprinkle with lemon juice and slowly stir in the crab meat until warm. Beat eggs and cream. Add chives, salt, pepper and cheese. Place crab-meat mixture in prebaked pie shell and pour the egg-and-cream mixture over it. Bake in moderate oven for about 45 minutes. Let stand for approximately 15 minutes before cutting as you would a pie. Serves 8.

Fish and Chips

(This is an easy two-step operation; first the chips and then the fish.)

CHIPS:

6 large baking potatoes
1 quart (about) oil, de-
pending upon the dimen-
sions of your deep fryer

Peel potatoes, wash and cut into about ¼- to ½-inch strips, preferably using a cutter that gives scalloped edges. Heat oil in deep fryer to 365°F., place chips in wire basket and fry *only* until they begin to turn color. Remove immediately to absorbent paper to drain while increasing temperature of oil to 370°F. Return chips to wire basket and fry until brown-crisp on the outside and creamy smooth on the inside. Transfer to baking pan lined with absorbent paper and place in heated oven to keep hot while preparing . . .

FISH:

2 lbs. fresh white-meat fish
fillets, ¼ to ½ inch
thick
1 cup flour

1 tsp. salt
1 tsp. pepper
1 cup milk

Slice fillets crosswise into 1-inch strips. Combine flour, salt and pepper. Dip fish in milk, then roll in flour mixture to lightly coat. Increase oil temperature in deep fryer to 375°F. Place fish strips in wire basket, lower into oil and fry until nicely browned and crisp. Transfer to absorbent paper to drain for a moment, then serve with chips. Serves 6.

VARIATION: Beer makes an interesting substitute for the milk.

Ned Pechairno's Baked Clams

36 hardshell clams
¼ cup finely chopped parsley, preferably Italian
2 garlic cloves, minced
¼ cup grated Parmesan
cheese

¼ tsp. black pepper, preferably freshly ground
½ tsp. oregano
¼ cup olive oil
¼ cup bread crumbs

Scrub clams under cold running water until shells shine. Dry. Place in skillet, cover and place over low heat until shells open just enough to permit a knife blade between the two sections. Separate shell with ordinary table knife so that clam remains in one half the shell. Discard the other half. Insert knife blade between clam and remaining shell and run it around to separate, but leave the clams in the shell. Arrange clams shell down in a baking pan and set aside. Mix parsley, garlic, cheese, pepper and oregano and sprinkle evenly on the clams. Then top with the oil and finally with bread crumbs. Bake 5 minutes in 425°F. oven. Serve immediately, 2, 4, 6 or 8 to a guest, depending upon their appetites.

NOTE: Follow the identical recipe for baked mussels, oysters or scallops. They all have their deliciously distinctive flavors.

Toots Shor's Shrimp Scampi

4 lbs. cleaned and de-
veined raw shrimp, split
½ cup melted butter
½ cup garlic, chopped

1½ cups onions, chopped
1½ cups shallots, chopped
⅔ cup parsley, chopped
5 ozs. dry white wine

Place shrimps in a very lightly greased flat pan. Stir melted butter into garlic, onion, shallots and parsley and sprinkle mixture over split raw shrimps. Bake in a 450°F. oven for 15 minutes, basting with wine. Serves 6.

Clam Aspic

1 10½-oz. can minced
  clams
Canned or bottled clam
  juice as needed
1 envelope unflavored gelatin
1 tb. cold water
1 small, ripe avocado
2 tbs. lemon juice
2 large hard-cooked eggs,
  peeled and cut into small
  cubes
1 or 2 stalks (small)

young, crisp celery,
  chopped
1 tsp. minced onion
4 pimiento-stuffed olives,
  sliced
¼ cup thick whipping
  cream (optional)
¾ cup mayonnaise
½ medium head of crisp
  lettuce, washed, dried
  and shredded
Paprika (optional)

Drain clams. Reserve and strain liquid. Add enough clam juice
to reserved liquid to make ¾ cup. Soften gelatin in 1 tb. cold water
for about 5 minutes. Heat clam juice to boiling, turn off heat and
stir in softened gelatin until it is well blended and completely
dissolved. Remove from stove and set aside. When cool, put in
refrigerator.

Lightly oil a 1-quart mold. Peel avocado and cut into small cubes.
Sprinkle immediately with lemon juice. Spread minced clams, eggs,
avocado, celery, onion and sliced olives over bottom of mold and
pour gelatin over them when it starts to thicken. Whip cream until
stiff, fold into mayonnaise and refrigerate. Chill mold preferably
overnight until firm. To unmold, dip mold ¾ of way up into hot
water. Don't leave it in for more than a few seconds, quickly wipe
moisture from bottom of mold to prevent dripping and invert onto
platter. If aspic is for a buffet, invert onto bed of shredded lettuce
which has been arranged on small serving platter. Garnish with
cream and mayonnaise sprinkled with a little paprika. If to be
served as individual salads, arrange lettuce on each small plate, lay
a slice of aspic on the lettuce, garnish with cream-and-mayonnaise
mixture and sprinkle with a little colorful paprika. Serves 6.

The Rose Restaurant's Lobster Americano

2 tbs. olive oil
1 clove garlic, chopped fine
2 1½-lb. lobsters, cracked, cleaned and cut into 2-inch pieces left in shell

1 small onion, chopped fine
2 tomatoes, chopped
¼ cup cognac
¼ cup white wine
6 tbs. tomato sauce

Heat oil in large skillet. Add garlic and stir once or twice. Add lobster and cook at high heat for 5 minutes, stirring occasionally. Reduce heat to medium, add onion and tomatoes and stir gently until onion browns. Add cognac and wine, stir, and add tomato sauce. Stir gently for 3 or 4 minutes. Reduce heat to low and let cook about 20 minutes more, stirring occasionally and adding water or soup stock if needed. Place lobster on platter and top with sauce from skillet. Serves 3 to 4.

Eel Matelote au Chateau Neuf du Pape

(Matelote d'anguille au Chateau Neuf de Pape)

(A *matelote* is a fish stew of the sort sailors' and fishermen's wives make. This one is a far cry from those simple everyday recipes and if you are ever able to get an eel or two, try this one of Chef Haentzler's and enjoy it.)

1½ to 2 lbs. eel
Butter
1 onion (medium-sized)
1 carrot (medium-sized)

1 clove garlic, crushed
Bouquet garni
Salt and pepper
4½ cups red wine

Skin, clean and wash the eel. Dry with a lint-free cloth and cut into 3-inch pieces. Butter a frying pan liberally and line with a layer of thinly-sliced onion and carrot. Cook over a slow flame for 15 to 20 minutes.

Add garlic and bouquet garni, season with salt and freshly ground pepper. Arrange pieces of eel on top and add enough wine to just cover the fish. Bring quickly to a boil, cover and simmer gently for 20 minutes. Remove eel and put aside in a deep dish, then strain the pan juices and pour over the fish.

20 small onions	Kneaded butter*
2 tbs. butter	Butter (about ¼ lb.)
Salt	Anchovy butter (optional)
Sugar	Watercress
20 button mushrooms	Fried croutons

Remove the eel, place on a plate, and measure the pan juices that were poured over the fish. Peel onions, scale and drain them. Cook them in 2 tbs. butter till golden. Season with a pinch each of salt and sugar, add mushrooms and sauté them for a few seconds before adding measured pan juices. Bring to a boil and add eel. Simmer for 2 to 3 minutes, then thicken with kneaded butter.* Allow 2 tbs. kneaded butter for each cup of juice. Add to the sauce half a tsp. at a time, stirring gently. Taste, add more seasoning if desired. Remove from heat and add remaining butter. (Anchovy butter may be substituted if desired.) Arrange on a heated plate, garnish with watercress and fried croutons. Serves 4.

---

* *Kneaded butter:* In French this is known as *beurre manie* and it is used as a thickener and to blend easily into sauces. To make it, blend to a smooth paste 5 tbs. butter and ¾ cup flour.

EGGS and
OTHER ANY-TIME THINGS

In this section you'll find recipes for dishes, like scrambled eggs, for instance, that through custom are mainly thought of as breakfast fare only—and some of them are—but which can be served and eaten at any time of the day or night. Not only that, the recipes you'll find here also can be excellent choices for serving to guests at luncheon or tea. Choose some of them, too, when a midnight snack is in order.

Speaking of eggs, here are a couple of pointers that will add immeasurably to both their health-packing qualities and to their flavor:

1. Buy only eggs that are refrigerated (unless you're one of those increasingly rare Americans who actually see the farmer remove them from the hen house) and refrigerate them the moment you get home.

2. Remove them from the refrigerator about half an hour before poaching or frying and let them stand, still in their shells, until they get to room temperature.

Scrambled Eggs

4 eggs	1 tb. butter or margarine
16 drops (about) Worcestershire sauce	

Remove eggs from refrigerator at least ½ hour before using and let stand at room temperature. Then break into bowl, add Worcestershire sauce and beat lightly with a fork. Warm frying pan on medium heat. Melt butter or margarine until it sizzles, taking care not to burn. Pour beaten eggs into pan and stir briskly with fork until desired doneness. Serve with salt and pepper to be added according to individual taste. Serves 2.

NOTE: Figure 4 drops of Worcestershire per egg for a starter and increase or decrease as personal taste dictates. I have a couple of friends who use 6 or 7 drops to the egg.

Olive and Chipped Beef Rarebit

1 cup medium white sauce	½ tsp. Worcestershire sauce
1 cup grated American cheese or, if you prefer a sharp cheese, 1 cup grated English cheddar	½ cup pitted ripe olives, coarsely chopped
½ tsp. salt	¼ lb. dried beef, shredded
¼ tsp. dry mustard	Paprika, for garnish

Heat white sauce in chafing dish over water pan or in top half of double boiler. Stir in cheese slowly until it melts. Stir in the seasonings and then the olives and beef, all the while stirring gently. It's done when smooth and creamy. Ladle liberally on buttered white toast, English muffin halves or large, round crackers. Sprinkle with paprika. Serves 4.

NOTE: Beef will be less salty if you place it in a pan before using, barely cover it with water and bring to a boil. Then drain well and proceed as above.

Cheddar and Worcestershire Spread

1 cup soft cheddar cheese	2 tsps. Worcestershire sauce
1 tb. butter or margarine	

Let cheese stand at room temperature for at least one hour. Then scrape into warm bowl, add butter or margarine and whip with a fork, adding Worcestershire to taste as you do so. When at consistency that is easily spread, place in refrigerator. Remove one hour before guests arrive and place on cocktail table, thus allowing it time to return to room temperature. Serve with crackers or toast bits. Makes about 24 canapés.

Chicken Rarebit

1 10½-oz. can condensed cream of chicken soup	¼ tsp. dry mustard
1 cup grated mild yellow American cheese or, if you prefer, 1 cup grated sharp cheddar cheese	¼ tsp. Worcestershire sauce
	Dash paprika
	½ cup cracker crumbs
	4 slices buttered toast
2 eggs, slightly beaten	Ripe olives, sliced

In chafing dish or double boiler, prepare soup according to directions on can. Add cheese and stir until blended and melted. Then add eggs, dry mustard, Worcestershire and paprika. Mix well and heat thoroughly. Fold in cracker crumbs just before serving on toast and garnish with olive slices. Serves 4.

Eggs Benedict

Proper timing is the secret ingredient in good eggs Benedict, so having everything ready to cook and all other things ready to eat before beginning your preparation is vital to the success of this recipe.

4 thin slices of precooked ham	4 egg yolks
4 eggs	1 cup sour cream
2 English muffins	1 pinch of salt
1 tb. butter	1 tsp. lemon juice

167

Put ham slices in large, heavy skillet and gently fry over medium heat. Put 4 eggs in poacher. Use fork to separate halves of 2 English muffins. Butter each half and put in broiler turned on to about 450°F. Heat water in bottom section of double boiler in which you will make hollandaise sauce. Don't let the water boil. Put egg yolks, sour cream, pinch of salt and lemon juice in top of double boiler. Heat slowly over steam, stirring constantly until thick and steaming hot but not boiling. Turn off heat and let stand.

Put 2 muffin halves on each of two plates. Put one slice of ham on each and top with a poached egg as soon as the eggs are done. Divide hollandaise sauce over the four eggs and serve at once. Serves 2 to 4.

The Lambs' German Apple Pancake

2 eggs, beaten	2 tsps. butter
1 cup milk	1 apple, cored, peeled and
1 pinch salt	sliced
1 pinch sugar	1 tsp. cinnamon sugar or
2 tbs. butter, melted	powdered sugar
½ cup flour	

Combine eggs, milk, salt, sugar, melted butter and flour. Beat into a batter for pancakes and set aside. Put 2 tsps. butter in 12-inch frying pan and, when butter is sizzling hot but not burning, add sliced apples and sauté for 2 minutes. Pour pancake batter over apples and put pan in oven preheated to 400°F. for 3 or 4 minutes. When pancake is lightly browned, remove to heated dinner plate, sprinkle with sugar and serve. Serves 1.

Omelet "21"

1 tsp. butter

2 eggs, well beaten

½ cup creamed chicken (chicken should be finely chopped)

1 tb. Mornay sauce

1 dash grated Parmesan cheese

Heat butter in omelet pan. When very hot but not smoking, pour in beaten eggs. Lift edges of omelet, letting raw egg run underneath to cook. If top is not done well enough for you by the time bottom of omelet is cooked, turn omelet over. Heat creamed chicken and place in center of omelet, roll up, top with Mornay sauce and sprinkle with grated Parmesan cheese. Brown under broiler and serve at once, while very hot. Serves 1 or 2.

OUTDOOR COOKING

Some Dos and Don'ts of Barbecuing Meats

Come late spring, which means summer, and every man's fancy
—at least men of my age—turns to thoughts of cooking outdoors.
Which means . . . barbecue! So here now a word for all to heed:

The biggest mistake people make in preparing barbecued meats
is to douse them with sauce before they have a chance to brown.
That may be a good way of preparing a burnt offering to one of
the netherworld gods, but it is not a good way of preparing meat—
be it pork, beef, lamb, fish or fowl—that either you or your guests
would want to eat. The reason is elementary: barbecue sauces are
sugary and sugar burns. So always remember, no matter what the
ingredients that go into your marinades, always wipe your meat
almost dry before putting it near the heat.

And make sure that you don't put foods on your grill until the
charcoal flames burn away and the coals turn gray with flecks of
red showing through. It's always a good idea, too, to rake your coals
away from the center of the pit. Then place the meat over the clear
spot and let the juices drip into it rather than onto the coals.

A steak should be grilled about four or five inches above the
coals. I start ribs at about the same distance. But, as with the steak,
when they are brown on both sides I drop them down an inch or
so, add some damp hickory chips to the coals, close the lid and let
the smoke slowly permeate the meat.

A big favorite in anyone's backyard is the charcoal-grilled hamburger. So much so that I'm sure there's no need for using up space
with recipes. Any seasoning that you happen to lay hands on will
lend a flavor that you may or may not want to try again. But, if
not, no harm is done because it seems that no matter what you do
to them, hamburgers taste good when cooked over charcoal.

However you may season your hamburger patties, I'd suggest
that you do what we do at our house—mix a teaspoonful of chopped
onion and three or four drops of Worcestershire sauce into each

171

of them. Those two simple additions are guaranteed to make every hamburger taste better.

And that's what outdoor cooking is all about.

Hickory-Smoke Barbecued Fish Steaks

6 fish steaks*, ½ to 1 inch thick
¼ cup melted butter
¼ cup olive oil
1 cup chili sauce or catsup
1 tb. Worcestershire sauce
6–10 drops Tabasco sauce, according to taste
Juice of 1 lemon
3 tbs. wine vinegar
1 clove garlic, finely chopped
2 tbs. grated onion
2 tsps. prepared mustard
Salt and paprika to taste
Hickory chips or powder

Dip fish steaks once or twice in cold salted water, pat thoroughly dry with lint-free cloth towel and set aside. Combine all other ingredients, except of course the hickory chips or powder, in a glass bowl. Add fish steaks and let stand 45 minutes, turning 2 or 3 times so that all surfaces are saturated. Meantime build your charcoal fire, sprinkling the coals preferably with hickory chips but with hickory powder if wood is not available, and let burn until coals are gray-hot. Remove fish steaks from marinade, pat lightly dry, fasten securely in a hinged, well-greased wire grill, and place about 4 inches above the coals. Barbecue 5 to 6 minutes on each side, basting frequently with the marinade sauce. Fish is done when it flakes easily with a fork. Serves 6.

Marinated Lamb Steak

4 lamb steaks, ½ to 1 inch thick
¾ cup olive oil
2 tbs. lemon juice
1 tsp. oregano
2 cloves garlic, sliced
Lemon juice
Crushed mint for garnish

* Any fish in season is fine.

Combine all ingredients (except lamb and mint) in a glass bowl and dip lamb steaks in mixture until well saturated. Spread lamb steaks on flat pan deep enough to hold marinade and small enough to fit into refrigerator.

Pour marinade over steaks. Let stand in refrigerator for 1 to 12 hours, the longer the better. Turn frequently. Remove steaks from marinade mixture, pat dry with lint-free cloth towel and broil over charcoal on an outdoor grill for ½ to 1 hour, depending upon taste and intensity of heat. Keep grill 3 or 4 inches above coals for first 10 minutes, then slowly raise to about 6 or 8 inches. Turn steaks 2 or 3 times and brush with marinade at least once. Remove from grill when done, sprinkle with lemon juice and garnish with crushed mint. Serves 4.

Shish Kebab, Armenian Style

½ cup olive oil	2 lbs. boneless lamb, cut
¼ cup lemon juice	into 1½-inch cubes
1 tsp. marjoram	3 green peppers,
1 tsp. thyme	quartered *
2 cloves garlic, crushed	3 sweet red peppers, quar-
½ cup chopped onion	tered *
½ cup chopped parsley	6 onions, sliced about
1 tsp. salt	¼ inch thick*
½ tsp. pepper	

Combine olive oil, lemon juice, marjoram, thyme, garlic, onion, parsley, salt and pepper in deep bowl. Mix well. Add meat, stir so each piece is nicely coated and marinate either by refrigerating overnight or by letting stand at room temperature for 2 or 3 hours. Turn occasionally. Then alternate meat cubes on skewers with pieces of green and red pepper and onion. To cook outdoors, place over charcoal. Indoors, lay skewers over 2-inch-deep baking pan and broil. In either case, turn several times and baste with the

* The amounts here are approximations, because the number of lamb cubes and skewer lengths are the determining factors.

marinade. Cooking time is about 10 to 20 minutes, depending on where you're broiling your kebabs and how well done you like them. When done, remove from skewers, brush with marinade and serve. Serves 6.

Mexican-Flavored Beef Kabobs

1 tb. olive oil
½ cup chopped onion
1 cup Chianti wine
¼ tsp. chili powder
½ tsp. oregano
½ tsp. cumin
½ tsp. ground cloves
½ tsp. cinnamon

1 garlic clove, minced
½ tsp. salt
½ tsp. pepper
1½ lbs. round steak, cut into 1½-inch cubes
5 sweet red peppers, quartered

Heat oil in skillet. Add onion and sauté until tender (do not brown). Add wine, chili powder, oregano, cumin, cloves, cinnamon, garlic, salt and pepper, cover and simmer 20 minutes. Meanwhile alternate pieces of meat and red pepper on skewer and, when sauce is done, brush liberally over kabobs. Broil over hot coals 10 to 20 minutes, depending upon desired degree of doneness, turning and basting occasionally. Kabobs may also be broiled in oven by placing skewers across 2-inch baking pan so that drippings fall into pan. Serve on a bed of rice. Serves 4 or more.

Barbecued Steak

½ cup olive oil
1 large clove garlic, crushed
¼ tsp. monosodium glutamate

6 strip steaks, each about 1½ inches thick*

* Strip steaks are also known as New York cut, Kansas City cut and loin-strip steaks. They usually weigh about 1¼ lbs. each. So 6 of them, while feeding only 6 hard-eating men, might feed 12 or more women and children.

Combine olive oil, garlic and monosodium glutamate. Lay steaks side by side in shallow pan, pour marinade over them and brush each side to coat thoroughly. Let stand several hours (preferably overnight) in refrigerator, turning often and brushing if necessary. Start charcoal fire 45 minutes before cooking is to begin. Pat steaks almost dry with lint-free towel. When coals are a red-flecked gray, set rack about 3 to 4 inches above them and add the steaks. Brown on each side, brush with marinade and broil 7 or 8 minutes on each side for medium, brushing several more times. Serves 6.

Easy-Do Barbecued Ribs

6 lbs. pork spareribs in 2   Hickory chips
  or 3 pieces
1 8-oz. bottle garlic salad
  dressing

Lay ribs in shallow pan. Pour half of the garlic dressing over each side, brushing to make sure the ribs are totally covered, and marinate overnight in refrigerator, turning and brushing several times. Start charcoal fire about 45 minutes before you start cooking. Remove ribs from refrigerator, pat almost dry with lint-free towel, and place on rack 3 to 4 inches above coals when red shows through the gray coals. Brown spareribs on both sides, brush with marinade, lower rack, sprinkle coals with damp hickory chips, close lid and cook about 1 hour or until done through, turning several times. Check for doneness by slitting into meat between bones. Test for tenderness by inserting fork tines. Ribs are done when meat is brown clear through and fork pierces flesh easily, not before. Serves 6.

Glazed Chicken, Hawaiian Style

2 2-lb. (about) broilers,
split in half lengthwise
½ cup salad oil
2 tsps. salt
½ tsp. pepper
1 cup crushed pineapple,
drained

2 tbs. syrup from pineapple
can
1 cup brown sugar
2 tbs. lemon juice
2 tbs. soy sauce
2 tbs. prepared mustard

Brush chicken well with oil, season with salt and pepper, and place on charcoal grill, skin-side up. Broil slowly about 20 to 30 minutes until well browned. Turn and cook the skin side for 15 minutes. Meantime prepare glaze by combining all other ingredients and stirring well. When skin side of chicken is nicely browned, brush both sides with glaze and broil another 10 minutes, turning and brushing twice. Pass extra glaze to those who want more while eating. Serves 4.

Charcoal-Roasted Beef

Hickory chips
4 lbs. bone-in chuck roast,
1½ inches thick
Salt and pepper to taste
2 stalks celery, sliced into
diagonal pieces
6 small carrots, cut into 3
or 4 pieces each

1 medium green pepper,
sliced into rings
2 medium onions, quar-
tered
2 tomatoes, cut into wedges

Add damp hickory chips to hot charcoal. Place roast on rack, brown about 7 minutes on each side and then place in center of 5-foot length of aluminum foil that has been folded double. Season roast with salt and pepper, cover the roast with the vegetables, wrap securely, return to rack about 4 inches above coals, and cook

1½ to 2 hours, turning 2 or 3 times. Transfer to serving dish, top with sauce (recipe follows) and serve. Serves 6 to 8.

SAUCE:

½ lb. butter or margarine, melted

4 tbs. Worcestershire sauce

4 tbs. catsup

3 drops Tabasco sauce, or to taste

Combine all ingredients in saucepan, bring to a boiling point and pour over meat.

Blockbuster Burgers

2 eggs

2 lbs. ground beef

2 tbs. Worcestershire sauce

1½ tsps. salt

½ tsp. garlic salt

¼ tsp. monosodium glutamate

Beat eggs lightly in bowl. Add meat and seasonings and mix thoroughly. Divide mixture into 3 parts and roll or pat each into a 7-inch circle. Leaving a 1-inch margin all around, spread ⅓ of the following recipe evenly over each half circle.

FILLING:

1 tb. prepared mustard, or more to taste

½ cup chopped onion

1 cup grated cheddar cheese, mild or sharp, to taste

½ cup pickle relish

1 tb. salad oil

Combine all ingredients, except oil, in bowl. Mix until well blended. Divide into 3 parts and spread as explained above. Fold beef over to a half-moon shape and press the 1-inch margins together tightly. Brush each half-moon with oil, taking care not to break while turning. Place each half-moon in long-handled wire charcoal grill basket and broil 4 to 5 inches above red-flecked coals, turning once or twice, until juice runs and they're done as you like them. Serves 4.

French Dip Steaks

8 minute steaks	2 tbs. Worcestershire sauce
¼ cup butter	2 loaves French bread
1 clove garlic, minced	Salt and pepper to taste
Juice of 1 lemon	

Start charcoal fire and, when flames are quite low, very quickly brown steaks on both sides. Remove from rack. When coals are gray flecked with red, tear off a sheet of aluminum foil large enough to cover rack and with enough left over to turn up edges about ½ inch. Place butter in this aluminum foil pan and, when melted, add garlic and squish around to blend well. Dip one side of steaks in garlic butter, turn, place other side down and broil 1 to 2 minutes. Then turn again and broil first side 1 to 2 minutes. Length of time will depend on doneness desired. Push steaks to one side of aluminum-foil pan, squeeze the lemon juice into the drippings, add Worcestershire sauce and blend. Then quickly run the steaks through the sauce, first one side and then the other. Set steaks aside. Cut bread in half and then cut each piece in half lengthwise. Dip each quarter-loaf bread in sauce, top each with a steak, season as desired with salt and pepper and serve. Serves 6 to 8.

Sliced Steak on Hot Dog Buns

(This is one of the Sterling Sisters' favorite swim-and-swallow sandwiches)

3 lbs. round, rump or chuck steak, about 2 inches thick	¼ lb. butter or margarine
	½ cup meat sauce
1½ tsps. unseasoned meat tenderizer	16 hot dog buns

Sprinkle both sides of steak evenly with tenderizer, poking holes with charcoal-grill fork into meat at ½-inch intervals and working some of the tenderizer into each hole. Dampen finger in water and rub over steak, thus providing just enough water to dissolve the tenderizer in the holes. (Be sure not to apply more water than can cling to your finger tip.) Dip finger often, however, to get enough water to cover all of steak. Start charcoal fire. Combine butter or margarine with meat sauce in saucepan. Beat and stir until well blended. When coals are a red-flecked gray, place steak on rack, brush with mixture, brown, turn and repeat. Then broil about 12 minutes on each side, figuring about 10 minutes per side for rare, about 15 minutes for well done. Remove to cutting board and slice diagonally across the grain. Slice buns, toast lightly, dip in marinade, place a slice of steak inside each and serve. Makes 16 such sandwiches, 2 each for the Sterling Sisters, ditto for Mother and Dad, and, if the steak slices aren't overly thick, leaves enough for later eating.

DESSERTS: Cakes, Pastries, and Even Garlic Bread

Iranian Peach Sundae

4 cups sliced peaches, preferably fresh and ripe
½ cup orange juice
3 tbs. honey

2 tbs. candied ginger, finely
chopped
1 pint vanilla ice cream

Combine all ingredients, except ice cream, in mixing bowl. Mix gently, cover and chill for several hours. Arrange in sherbet glasses with alternating layers of ice cream. Serves 8.

NOTE: A good trick for assuring that fresh peaches will hold their color is to quickly dip the sliced fruit in lemon juice.

Peachy Cherry Berry Compote

1 10-oz. pkg. frozen raspberries
1 1-lb. can pitted Bing
cherries

2 tbs. sherry wine
3 large red-ripe peaches,
halved and pitted

Remove wrappings from raspberries while still stiffly frozen and place berries in bowl. Pour cherries, undrained, over the frozen berries, add sherry wine and let stand one hour. Place one peach half in each of 6 dessert dishes and top with cherry-berry mixture. The berries should have crystals clinging to them. If not, cut down on chilling time next time. Serves 6.

181

Spiked Grapefruit for Kids

2 grapefruits	¼ tsp. nutmeg
1½ tbs. butter	¼ tsp. cinnamon
1½ tbs. light brown sugar	

Cut grapefruits in half, remove seeds and separate pulp from membranes. Blend butter, sugar and spices and dot over grapefruit halves. Bake in shallow pan at 375°F. about 15 minutes. Serves 4.

Spiked Grapefruit for Grownups

2 grapefruits	½ tb. brandy
1 tb. butter	¼ tsp. nutmeg
½ tb. honey	¼ tsp. cinnamon

Cut grapefruits in half, remove seeds and separate pulp from membranes. Blend all other ingredients and spread over grapefruit halves. Bake in shallow pan at 375°F. about 15 minutes. Serves 4.

Plum Crunch

3 lbs. plums, cut up and pitted	½ tsp. salt
¼ cup brown sugar	½ tsp. cinnamon
1 cup flour	1 egg, beaten
1 cup granulated sugar	½ cup melted butter or margarine

Combine plums and brown sugar and place in shallow baking pan. Sift flour, sugar, salt and cinnamon into a bowl, add the egg and whip with fork until crumbly. Pour evenly over the plum-and-brown-sugar mixture. Drizzle with melted butter or margarine and bake in preheated 375°F. oven about 40 to 45 minutes or until lightly browned. Spoon into dessert dishes and top with whipped cream or ice cream. Serves 8.

Tipsy Trifle

1 18-oz. (about) package
yellow cake mix
½ tsp. almond extract
1 20-oz. (about) can pie
apples, well drained

½ cup light brown sugar
¼ cup sherry wine
1 1¾-oz. package vanilla
pudding
2¼ cups milk

Bake the cake in pan 13 × 9 × 2 inches according to package directions but adding almond extract to the batter. When done, remove to rack to cool. Combine apples, brown sugar and sherry wine in a bowl, mix well and let stand 1 hour, stirring occasionally. Combine vanilla pudding and milk in saucepan, bring to a boil at medium heat and then stir in apple mixture. Shut off heat and let stand while cutting cake into serving-size squares. Spoon warm apple mixture over top of each and serve.

VARIATIONS: Toasted almond slivers sprinkled on top of all adds a tasty touch. If you don't mind where your calories come from or how many, you also might try topping Tipsy Trifle with whipped cream.

Swiss Apple Cake

3 eggs
1¼ cups sugar
1 cup oil
½ cup lukewarm water
1 tsp. vanilla extract
¼ tsp. salt

2½ cups flour
3 tsps. baking powder
8 medium apples, cored,
peeled, halved and sliced
1 tb. butter or margarine
1 tsp. cinnamon

Break eggs into large bowl and beat until thick. Add 1 cup sugar and continue beating until absorbed. Add oil, water, vanilla and salt. Beat until well blended. Add flour and baking powder and continue beating until thoroughly mixed. Grease a 13 × 9 × 2-inch baking pan well with butter or margarine, pour in half the batter

183

and spread apple slices over all. Combine cinnamon with remaining
¼ cup sugar and sprinkle mixture over apples. Pour the remaining
batter over all and bake in 350°F. oven for 1 hour.

Cherry Pudding

PUDDING BATTER:

2 tbs. shortening	½ tsp. salt
1 cup sugar	2 tsps. baking powder
2 cups all-purpose flour	1 cup milk

Cream shortening and mix with sugar. Sift flour, salt and baking
powder and mix with shortening-sugar combination, alternating
with milk as you add the flour. Beat until smooth and pour into
greased baking dish. Then prepare . . .

TOPPING:

1 quart canned, unpitted sour cherries	½ cup sugar
1 cup cherry juice from can	1 tb. butter

Combine all ingredients in a pot. Cook until it starts to simmer.
Then pour over batter in greased baking dish and bake in a moderate 350°F. oven for 30 minutes. Serves 8.

NOTE: This basic pudding batter can be used for just about
any pudding that you care to make, provided, of course, that it calls
for a cake-type base.

Brandied Pineapple

1 pint heavy cream	2 tbs. brandy
6 small pineapples	1 tb. sugar

Pour cream into mixing bowl and place in refrigerator to chill. Peel and core pineapple and then dice. Combine brandy and sugar and stir to dissolve. Remove cream from refrigerator, add brandy to the chilled cream and beat until stiff but not dry. Stir in the pineapple cubes and serve. Serves 6.

N O T E : If you're an expert or willing to try anything once, remove pineapple cores from shells, taking pains not to pierce them, and set them aside until the brandied pineapple is prepared. Then spoon the mixture back into the shells for serving. It's quite decorative.

Swedish Pancakes, à la Sterling

1 cup flour	Butter, as needed
2 tbs. sugar	10 to 12 tsps. your favorite
¼ tsp. salt	jam or jelly
3 eggs, beaten	Powdered sugar
3 cups milk	

Sift flour, sugar and salt into a bowl. Mix in eggs and milk gradually, stirring slowly until well blended, and let stand about 2 hours. Heat an 8-inch or 10-inch pancake griddle and lubricate lightly with butter. When butter sizzles gently but does not brown, pour pancake batter (making sure it is free of lumps) onto griddle until it is thinly coated. When pancake is lightly browned on bottom, turn carefully with a spatula and brown the other side. Place on warm platter and repeat. While second pancake is browning on griddle, spread a generous tsp. of your favorite preserve on portion of finished pancake nearest you, lift edge gently and roll loosely away from you. Serve topped with butter and powdered sugar. Makes 10 to 12 pancakes.

N O T E : The traditional Swedish pancake is done in a special pan that turns out cakes no more than 3 inches in diameter. The Sterling clan prefers them large and rolled up like blintzes.

Garlic Bread

¼ lb. butter or margarine
½ tsp. garlic powder
½ tsp. celery seed

½ tsp. oregano
1 loaf Italian or French
bread

Let butter or margarine stand at room temperature until soft enough to work with easily. Combine garlic powder, celery seed and oregano. Blend mixture thoroughly into the soft butter with a fork and let stand at room temperature for 30 minutes. Cut bread into 1-inch pieces, taking care not to slice through bottom crust. Spread garlic butter generously on both sides of each joined slice, wrap entire loaf in aluminum foil and bake in preheated moderate (350°F.) oven for 30 minutes. Remove from oven, turn down foil to form a basket and place on table while still piping hot. Italian bread should serve 4 to 6, French bread 8 to 10.

NOTE: A sliced garlic clove may be substituted for the garlic powder and the slices removed from the bread before it is wrapped and put into oven.

Apple Nut Bread

2 cups biscuit mix
1 cup rolled oats
¾ cup sugar
1 tsp. baking powder
¼ tsp. cinnamon
¼ tsp. nutmeg

¼ tsp. salt
1 cup grated, pared apples
1 cup chopped walnuts, or
your choice of nuts
1¼ cups milk
1 egg, well beaten

Combine biscuit mix, rolled oats, sugar, baking powder, cinnamon, nutmeg and salt, then stir in grated apple and chopped nuts. Combine milk and egg, add to the apple-nut mixture and beat vigorously for ½ minute. Place mixture into a well-greased 9 × 5 × 3-inch loaf pan and bake at 350°F. for 1 hour. Serves 8 to 10.

Grapefruit Meringue Pie

½ grapefruit
4 tbs. flour
4 tbs. cornstarch
1½ cups sugar
1 tsp. salt
2¼ cups boiling water
3 egg yolks, beaten

½ cup grapefruit juice
Juice of 1 lemon
1 tsp. butter
Crust for 8- or 9-inch pie
  (see recipe below)
Meringue (see recipe
  below)

Remove grapefruit, set pulp aside for use another day some other way, and grate rind. Mix flour, cornstarch, sugar and salt in heavy pan. Gradually add boiling water, stirring constantly on high heat until thick. Turn heat low, add egg yolks and cook 2 more minutes. Remove from heat, add grapefruit rind, grapefruit and lemon juice and butter. Stir until well blended. Cool and spread evenly in baked pie shell or graham cracker crust, top with meringue (recipes for all 3 follow) and bake, in order to brown the meringue, in 300°F. oven for 15 to 18 minutes.

BAKED PIE SHELL (FOR 8-INCH OR 9-INCH PIE PAN)

1 cup sifted, all-purpose
  flour
½ tsp. salt

⅓ cup shortening
4–5 tbs. cold water

Mix flour and salt, cut in shortening with knife or pastry blender, slowly mix in water. Remove to floured board in a ball, flatten with hand and roll out lightly to almost ⅛-inch thickness with cloth-covered rolling pin, first making sure that cover has been rubbed with flour. Keep rounding pastry edges to roll into circle 2 inches larger than bottom of pan. Quickly pinch edges together if pastry should break while rolling. To transfer to pie pan, fold in half for easy handling, then unfold and spread to loosely cover bottom and sides of pan. Do not stretch. Pierce shell liberally with fork on both bottom and sides and bake 12 to 15 minutes or until golden brown in oven that has been preheated to 450°F.

GRAHAM CRACKER CRUST (FOR 8-INCH OR 9-INCH PIE PAN)

12 graham crackers   ½ cup melted butter
⅓ cup sugar

Combine all ingredients and mix well. Press firmly into greased pan and chill about 45 minutes or until set.

MERINGUE (FOR 8-INCH OR 9-INCH PIE)

3 egg whites   Scant ⅓ tsp. cream of tartar
¼ tsp. salt   6 tbs. sugar

Remove eggs from refrigerator and immediately, while still cold, separate the whites and set the yolks aside for use another day. Pour whites into small, deep bowl and let warm to room temperature. Beat, preferably with electric mixer, until stiff and foamy; add salt and cream of tartar. When mixture can hold soft peaks, add sugar, 2 tbs. at a time, and blend well before adding more. Meringue is ready for use when it has been beaten long enough to hold stiff peaks.

Raisin Honey Cookies

¾ cup honey   1 tsp. salt
¾ cup sugar   1 tsp. cinnamon
¾ cup butter or margarine   ½ tsp. baking soda
1 egg   1 cup seedless raisins
2 cups sifted flour   2 cups raw rolled oats

Thoroughly cream honey, sugar, butter and egg. Sift flour, salt, cinnamon and baking soda and stir into creamed mixture. Mix in raisins and oats and drop heaping teaspoonfuls onto lightly greased cookie sheets. Bake on top shelf of preheated 375°F. oven 12 to 14 minutes, until lightly browned. Let cool on racks. Makes about 48 cookies.

Gingerbread Men

1 tsp. ginger	½ cup brown sugar,
1 tsp. ground cloves	packed
1½ tsps. cinnamon	½ cup granulated sugar
½ tsp. nutmeg	1 large egg
½ tsp. salt	½ cup molasses
½ tsp. baking powder	2½ cups sifted flour
½ cup shortening	Raisins

Combine ginger, cloves, cinnamon, nutmeg, salt and baking powder and set aside. Place shortening, brown sugar and granulated sugar in mixing bowl and cream well. Add egg and molasses, mix well and then blend in the ginger mixture and sifted flour. When thoroughly blended, wrap the cookie batter in wax paper and chill about 2 hours or until firm enough to handle. Then roll out on a lightly floured board to about a ⅛-inch thickness and cut into gingerbread men shapes with a 6-inch cutter that is available in almost any store that stocks kitchen utensils. Place on lightly greased baking sheets, add eyes, nose, mouth and coat buttons by pressing raisins into dough, and bake in preheated oven at 350°F. 10 or 12 minutes. Cool thoroughly before eating. Makes 12 gingerbread men, 2 per Sterling Sister.

Citrus Chiffon Pie in Nut Crust

½ cup lemon juice
¼ cup orange juice
¼ cup lime juice
½ tsp. grated lemon rind
½ tsp. grated orange rind
4 egg yolks
1¾ cups sugar
Dash salt

1 tb. (1 envelope) un-
    flavored gelatin
¼ cup cold water
3 or 4 drops yellow food
    coloring, optional
4 egg whites
Nut crust (recipe follows)

Combine juices, rinds, egg yolks, 1½ cups sugar and salt in top of double boiler. Cook and stir constantly. Meanwhile, in another dish combine gelatin with cold water and allow to stand to soften. When double-boiler mixture coats a spoon it is done. Remove from heat and stir in coloring (if desired) and softened gelatin. Stir until dissolved. Chill until mixture will form mounds when dropped from a spoon. Beat egg whites frothy, slowly beat in the remaining ¼ cup sugar and continue beating until glossy smooth and able to hold peaks. Fold into citrus-and-gelatin mixture and refrigerate another 30 minutes while making . . .

NUT CRUST

1 or 2 tsps. butter
1½ cups ground nuts of
   your choice

¼ cup sugar

Grease 9-inch pie pan lightly but completely with butter. Mix nuts and sugar thoroughly. Press mixture over sides and bottom of pie plate, the butter serving as the mortar that holds things in place. Spoon refrigerator mixture (previous recipe) into shell, top with whipped cream if desired, and either serve or continue chilling until time for dessert. Serves 8.

Ruby Wren's Raisin Scones

2 cups all-purpose flour, sifted	2 tsps. cream of tartar
½ cup sugar	½ cup shortening
¾ tsp. salt	½ cup raisins
1 tsp. baking soda	¼ cup milk
	2 eggs, slightly beaten

Sift together flour, sugar, salt, baking soda and cream of tartar. Work in shortening with pastry blender or knife until it has cracker-crumb consistency. Add raisins, milk and eggs and mix. Divide in two, turn each part onto floured board and roll about ¼ inch thick. Cut into triangles, diamonds or circles and "bake" on lightly but well-greased griddle until brown on both sides. Serve hot or cold, plain or with jam, jelly, marmalade, butter or honey. Yield: about 24.

N O T E : Griddle-baked scones can be made on any source of heat: hot plate as Ruby did, top of stove, campfire, charcoal grill or chafing dish. Baked-in-oven scones should be rolled about ½-inch thick, placed on floured and greased cookie sheet and baked in 400–425°F. preheated oven about 15 minutes or until golden brown.

Jane DeFreitas' Pound Cake

(Basic recipe for plain, lemon breakfast, mocha-iced, or strawberry shortcake)

1 cup butter	½ tsp. mace
2 cups granulated sugar	½ tsp. salt
5 eggs	⅔ cup milk
2½ cups cake flour	1 tsp. lemon extract
2½ tsps. baking powder	Icing (optional)

Cream butter thoroughly. Then add sugar, a little at a time, beating it into the butter until mixture is light and fluffy. Add eggs, one at a time, and beat. Combine flour, baking powder, mace and salt. Mix these dry ingredients and milk alternately into batter, adding a little at a time, scraping bowl sides and beating thoroughly. Stir in lemon extract and pour cake batter into tube pan lined with wax paper. (Use well-buttered layer pans if cake will be used for strawberry shortcake.) Bake cake for 1 hour in oven preheated to 350°F. Do not open oven door. Test with skewer for doneness. If not finished at the end of an hour, bake 5 or 10 minutes longer. When done to a golden brown, top of cake usually rises above top of tube pan. Wax paper may be left on until ready to serve or ice.

MOCHA ICING:

¾ cup butter
1 pinch salt
¼ cup cocoa
3½ cups sifted confectioners sugar
¼ cup cold strong coffee (made doubly strong by adding 2 tsps. instant coffee to ¼ cup of hot regular coffee)
3 tbs. (more or less) of cream for thinning icing to desired thickness

Let butter stand at room temperature until soft. Add pinch of salt and beat until fluffy and creamy. Mix cocoa into 1 cup of sugar. Stir a little at a time into butter. Gradually add coffee and sugar-cocoa mixture into butter, alternating between the two ingredients and using half of each. At this point you should have a very creamy icing which you may wish to use as is, or with a little more sugar as a filling for layer cakes not being used for strawberry shortcakes. Taste, to see if more cocoa or coffee is desired. For icing on outside of cake, continue to add remaining sugar and cream as necessary to make a nice spreading consistency.

NOTE: If cake is to be used uniced or as a breakfast cake, grate the rind of a lemon into batter at the same time lemon extract is added.

PARTY PUNCH

Champagne Punch

2 large, ripe pineapples, peeled and diced
32 maraschino cherries, drained
3 6-oz. cans frozen lemonade diluted by 6 cans water

½ cup curaçao
2 cups brandy
2 cups rum
3 quarts champagne, chilled

Divide diced pineapple and maraschino cherries into the ice cube divisions in two 16-cube trays. Carefully pour lemonade into the two trays and freeze. Combine curaçao, brandy and rum; pour into a large glass punchbowl and chill. Shortly before serving, stir in champagne and frozen fruit cubes. Serves 40 to 50.

INDEX

195

Index

Index